Terry!

If it was easy it would have been done.

Say God size vision's multi-generational & its steps impossible to its completion.

Here is to the crazy ones that dare to dream!

**ISBN-10:** 0-9965687-5-1

**ISBN-13:** 978-0-9965687-5-3

Dr. John A. King

# #DEALWITHIT:
# LIVING WELL WITH PTSD

*Next Foundation Press*

# Praise for *#dealwithit*

"It's f*cking brilliant! "

Kathysue Dorey
*Creative Leadership Facilitator and Speaker*

"[Dr. King's] honesty is rare in this field, and it's nice to get a vibe that you are talking to a real person—he puts his story out there very candidly. *#dealwithit* explains very complex concepts very simply. It has a good voice and an easy flow, which make a relatively quick read. If you are interested in dealing with your own PTSD, or just in the topic in general, I highly recommend this book."

Jason Walter
*Venthouse Counseling*

"I thought I dealt with a lot of my issues and anxieties when I got out, but I hadn't. Reading this book has encouraged me to get on with the recovery process in my life—to stop procrastinating, and just deal with it and move forward. It's long overdue for me."

Lcpl Xavier W. Webb
*U.S. Marine*

"This book is incredible for anyone who doesn't know what Post Traumatic Stress Disorder is, or what it's like to live with PTSD. There are passages that will have you laughing, then others that will pull emotion from you...I was diagnosed in 2017, and I really couldn't be happier having found this book."

Matthew Heneghan
*Canadian Armed Forces Medic*

"Accessible, relatable...the candor and humor allowed me to access parts of myself that I wouldn't have been able to if it were written from a clinical standpoint. *#dealwithit* breaks through the stigma, that separation that [trauma sufferers] often experience. It makes them feel like they are not alone, and others understand what they are going through. I firmly believe in our ability to self-heal, and this book is definitely a methodology to make that happen."

Rick Scarpello
*This is Men's Therapy*

"This book is amazing even if you aren't struggling with PTSD. If you know someone who is...it gave me so much empathy that I don't think I would have been capable of getting to on my own. It opened my eyes and...gave me the tools to cope as someone on the outside watching [PTSD] happen to someone else. You also don't have to have a doctorate in psychology to understand this book. It's very well done, very intelligently written and so practical."

Amber Courtot
*Photographer*

# #DEALWITHIT

LIVING WELL WITH PTSD

DR. JOHN A. KING

# Dedication

To the men and women who stood and walked with me;

To the voice on the other end of the phone, the light that guided me home;

Thank you.

# Forward

Let's start with some of my favorite quotes from *#dealwithit* (there are many):

*"I am resilient."*

*"What the hell is normal anyway?"*

*"A victim's already lost his battle. I have just begun to fight."*

*"People cannot see the mental illness and they don't take time to understand it."*

*"I am not my past. I am my future."*

*"Whether you believe you can or whether you believe you can't, you are right."*

BUT my all time favorite is: *"The heart is an emotional memory of what happens in your life."*

The fascinating thing about this book is understanding John's journey from his view point. As a physician, I know the clinical

aspects and the whole dopamine, serotonin, norepinephrine interaction. For me it was amazing seeing how one man has applied all this in his life, and how he has taught himself to heal.

At the end of each chapter, John's wife, Melissa, shares her perspective. This element is very important, as it illustrates the struggles and victories that the family members and friends of people with PTSD go through.

SO, why did I love this book...I loved it because although my clinical brain knew the medical principles around PTSD, my heart had not yet caught up to how they translated to real living. Dr. King, by telling his story, his struggles and triumphs, has brought it back to me full circle.

I firmly believe that we all are a sum of our past experiences and future hopes, but our will to work hard and OWN IT is what makes us unique and bold.

Sincerely,

Katarina Lindley, D.O. FACOFP

# Contributors

## MELISSA KING

Melissa has a Bachelor of Science in Marketing and completed her graduate study in Applied Economics at Clemson University. Since then she has gone on to get her Ph.D in multiple fields – including 'Keeping Me Alive.' She is a proven subject-matter expert to a very limited audience of one (back the f*ck off fella), and is most brilliant at hold handing, cuddling, and making me smile.

I love this picture of us (I wanted to put in the picture from her 40th birthday party, she looked hot, but she thought I looked too much like Ron Jeremy - the LMFAO 'Sexy And I Know it' version). This was one of the first times we went on a date. I asked her to meet me at a little airfield and told her we were going to lunch at the airport cafe. What I didn't tell her was that it was an hour's flight away and I was doing the flying. It was a $300 hamburger and totally worth it.

# KATHYSUE DOREY

After I sent Kathysue the first draft of #dealwithit and got this response, "This is f*cking brilliant," I thought I might just have my editor. When I found out that she and her husband agreed on the choice of their family home based on a garage that would be turned into his man cave, the deal was sealed.

The bonus rounds for me came when I found out she was so incredibly qualified – I mean credited out the wazoo: Master of Science in Creativity, Leadership and Innovation; Executive Coach through the Center for Educational Leadership; Pure Krav Maga Senior Master Instructor; and Founder/Lead Facilitator of The Freedom Legacy Impact Study, which conducts Empirical research with domestic violence and sexually assaulted survivors.

Through the eyes of an advocate and academic, Kathysue saw what I had accomplished; and realized that #dealwithit was groundbreaking in its recounting of the organic and intuitive way I discovered and applied learning principles from over 20 different methodologies/pathways. She says #dealwithit will give profound insight into the brain's ability to creatively problem-solve and heal its self from myriad forms of trauma.

# Contents

Author's note: I don't find that life is linear, and this story certainly isn't. So in the table of contents, I wanted to provide some chronological context for those of you who might find it useful. The contents format is as follows:

## CHAPTER TITLE

Section Title                                    Page #

*Chronological Context*

# #DEALWITHIT

# EPILOGUE

# APPLIED PSYCHOLOGICAL METHODOLOGIES/ PATHWAYS (JOHN'S TOOLBOX)

# INTRODUCTION

# A Beginning of Sorts

House blowing up builds character.

—Deadpool

Life is not chronological.

Life is a collection of experiences, a tapestry woven over time.

I find it impossible to tell my story, this story, starting at the chronological beginning. Because what I want to convey doesn't start there. So I'll start at what will probably end up being a middle-ish point, then head back to the beginning, and then move forward to my today. Not the today you are reading in, but the

today I am writing in. It's important to me that you understand that. Why? Because long ago I made the decision that my past would never define me; I would only allow it to refine me.

In the coming pages, I talk about my struggles and victories, the battles I have lost and the ones I am in the process of winning. *Parts will be repeated ... parts will be repeated ... parts will be repeated ...* Why? Because one aspect of Post Traumatic Stress Disorder (PTSD) can affect many areas of a person's life. For example, the inability to process fear and emotion might affect one's ability to be in crowds. This same issue can affect someone's sex life. I want to discuss and approach these topics differently, but there will be some commonality. So I am giving you a heads up ... *parts will be repeated.*

For some of you, this book may seem choppy and sarcastic, more like a Deadpool comic than a Hemingway novel, and that's okay. My name isn't Dr. FirstnameOnly and this isn't my 47 secrets to successful anything. If you need an analogy, think of this book as duct tape for the soul. I don't see myself as a static person. I am a work in progress, and you need to read this book like that. Start where you need to. Read what you want to. It's like breakfast cereal for dinner. It doesn't really matter because it all ends up in the same place anyway.

Here is my first thought for you: if I can make it, if my past and my present can be building blocks for future purpose – so can yours. I am living proof that if you still have breath, there is still a chance for any situation, no matter how bad, to turn around for good.

When you've finished reading this book, drop me an email; I'd love to hear from you. Why? Because I am incredibly caring? No. Because I feel very insecure and vulnerable about this whole thing. I paid an incredible price to relive and retell this on paper, and I need to hear that it was worth it.

**dealwithit@nextfoundation.org**

– John

# Tuck Your Chin and Throw Punches

At one of the lowest points in my life, I held on, not to my favorite Bible verse or inspirational quote, but to the words of my old boxing coach, Steve Goin.

When the fight took place, I was feeling every one of my 46 years; and my opponent, aka "the kid," was a fresh 23 thinking he was invincible, as we all did at that age. I was scared, but not worried. I had two things the kid didn't have: I had Coach and I had the Sweat Shed. Coach won his second USA kickboxing title at 47 with a broken collarbone. The Sweat Shed was an old brick building we turned into a boxing gym right behind the church.

We had a full-size ring, bags hanging from the roof and no A/C. In the summer it got to 115 degrees. In the winter, you froze your

arse off and by the time you got warm, you went home. The kid came from a climate-controlled gym at a constant 72 degrees, with mirrors on the wall and piped-in motivation music and speeches. They had photos of Sylvester Stallone; we had photos of Rocky. We trained 3-minute rounds; they trained 2-minute rounds. We trained because we loved to; they trained because they got paid. My coach was 60-something with a six-pack and could still do full splits; their coach was 20-something and carried a boom box so the Kid didn't hurt his hands.

[You need to have *Eye of The Tiger* playing while you read this part.]

In my corner, before the first round, Coach told me:

*"He is younger and faster than you, that's just a fact. But he is cocky. He has travelled all this way and brought his minders so they could see 'the champ' beat on the old preacher. You're nothing to him but a practice session before he goes to his 'real fight' next month.*

*So you will take everything he gives you for the first two minutes. You will absorb every blow and every punch. I don't want you throwing anything. I want you ducking and weaving and trying to get your old arse down and out of the way. Because if he hits you; he is going to hurt you. He will be fast, and he will throw everything at you from the bell to try and get you down in the first 30 seconds. But here is the thing: he only knows how to do that for two minutes because he only trains for 2-minute rounds. When we hit two minutes, he will want to stop. He is used to stopping. He will not have even expected the round to go past*

*two minutes; but you see, that's the beauty of the match being in our gym. YOU have another 60 seconds to go.*

*Remember, you've trained harder than he has. You've trained longer than he has. You're more disciplined than he is.*

*Preacher, you have lived through shit that he has no idea about.*

*So I want you to suck it up, and when I yell, 'GO!' I want you to TUCK YOUR CHIN AND THROW PUNCHES, and you'd better not stop till the bell rings, or I'll kick your arse myself."*

Last I saw that kid, he was throwing up behind the gym as I walked to the car. He would go on to take the Middleweight Everest Boxing Title the next week, but on that Thursday night, I kicked his arse.

*How did I manage to do that against a kid half my age?*

Because like Mona said, I AM RESILIENT.

Confused because you don't know who Mona is? Don't be. Relax; that's that whole tapestry thing I was telling you about.

Mona is the therapist I saw for three weeks, about four years after I fought the Kid. But I never would have made it to Mona who told me I were resilient, if Coach hadn't shown me what that meant in a way I could understand.

Similarly, what you read today may not be useful to you today. But I promise you, somewhere in your tomorrow, it will come in handy.

## CHAPTER ONE

# The Story So Far

## OH CRAP, WHAT HAVE I DONE?!

The theater was packed. For the first time tonight, the investors, cast, crew, and their families would see the completion of two years of hard work with the documentary *Stopping Traffic*. Anticipation was building. Up to this point, *Stopping Traffic* had won six awards with talk of more to come. Some said it was the best documentary on human trafficking they ever saw. Some said it was too much, too hard, and too real for anyone to ever watch. Some said it might get nominated for an Oscar.

After we shot the original footage in my apartment, we wondered for months if I were even going to be in the film. The crew had travelled all over the world for over a year and interviewed 70 different people. I blew it off and put it down as another one of those things that never seemed to work out for me. Life was shitty

and this was just another turd on the pile. At best, I might be in the film for a couple of minutes.

We found out later that when the executive producer and the editor saw the raw footage, they thought my story tied all the elements together and formed a backbone for the movie. They didn't just use a small piece of my story; they used all of it. When I first saw the film's rough-cut on a laptop, I went from a 53-year-old man to an 11-year-old boy the moment it started. It took me a week to recover. For weeks now, Mel and I have been trying to figure out ways to help me see it again in front of a crowd of people.

When I told one of my military mates about shooting the film and then going to see it, he put it this way, "You're FUCKING mad. That's like taking all the worst bits of every battle I have ever been in, and not only reliving it, but also showing that shit to the world for all time. Every motherfucker on the planet is going to come up and want to comment on your life and pat your fucking head. Bro, you got to stop that, you'll go FUCKING crazy!"

I knew he cared for us and FUCKING loved me, but what was I to do? For years, I suffered in silence because no one would talk to me about my experiences. Apparently, men don't get raped and all teenage boys "enjoy having sex with older women," even if the women were their mother and her friends. Someone had to call bullshit on all of this, and I couldn't see anyone else with his hand up. So I thought, "Bugger it, I'll do it." But it sucked, and it continues to suck every time I see the movie or talk about my story.

The showing for the cast and crew was in Santa Monica, CA. Mel and I got to the theatre early and milled around. No one knew

who I was. People were asking me for directions, where the toilet was, and if I could get them "popcorn." It was surreal. For those brief moments, I felt normal, but I knew that wouldn't last. I had agreed to do a Q&A at the end of the film, and I was about to go from the "popcorn guy" to the freak on the screen with the shitty past.

But that was yet to come; it was still a 72 *long* minutes away. And yet, here I was, the "popcorn guy," with my lap covered in popcorn because I kept missing my mouth; squeezing Mel's hand so tight that her engagement ring was cutting off the blood to her fingers … waiting …

… the lights came down.

And I started to cry as I heard my voice say, "I started having sex at the age of 4. I watched my father put bread and water in my mother's vagina, and I engaged in an oral act."

AND IT ALL CAME FLOODING BACK.

And all I remember thinking was, "OH CRAP, WHAT HAVE YOU DONE, MATE?"

When the screening ended, I remember walking to the front of the room as that feeling I had lived with for years came back. I felt stained, soiled, "like excrement on a sacred altar." It took a while for the room to warm — *Stopping Traffic* is a heavy watch. Our emcee, Jeannie Mai, stood and cried and said thank you to the producers. Someone else stood and told Karla, whose story is featured as well, and me, that they were sorry it happened to us. We thanked them all and waited. Then it happened. Someone

stood and said the thing I didn't realize I longed to hear; the thing I needed to hear and made all of this pain and recall worthwhile: "Dr. King, I am really pissed off about this, and I promise you, I will stay pissed off."

And in that moment, when I heard those words, I knew it was worth it.

By mustering the courage to tell my story, I knew I'd make people extraordinarily angry; I only hoped however, that they'd be angry enough to do something to help and/or protect a child.

#DEALWITHIT

# RAIN

i was young when it happened old when he left
he came when it rained

he said
lie still
hold still
i'll do it
don't struggle
no one will know

but they can all tell
they see it
they know.
i'm defiled
    soiled
    smeared like excrement
    on a sacred altar

he came telling me it would make me a man
he came telling me it wouldn't last long
he came telling me it wouldn't hurt

then why does it still ache? why does it never stop?

Taken from *No Working Title: a Life in Progress* by Dr. John A. King, available at www.drjohnaking.com.

i lay awake
pretending to sleep hating the nights dreading the dreams

puddles
in the corners of my soul

fearing the rain

longing for sunshine.

I can't get there on my own

You can't leave me here alone

I'm just trying to do what's right

Oh a man ain't a man 'less he's fought the fight

—Kings of Leon, *Walls*

## WHEN THE WALLS CAME TUMBLING DOWN

My life started to crumble in 2008. I lost my marriage, became estranged from my kids, shipwrecked a career, found my health devastated, and my peace of mind was shattered — not because of something I did, but because of something done to me.

When the memories came back, they came back like a flood, one sunny Thursday afternoon at about 3 o'clock. I had been sitting in my study; a wonderful, cedar-clad shed nestled in a wooded two acres in the middle of a very comfortable, suburban city in the Dallas/Fort Worth area of Texas.

[My childhood, to this point, had been a collection of memories, scattered in most parts, unconnected for me. These memories were like still frames of grief; sad things that I wouldn't wish upon anyone. Sad things that were difficult to think about, and I did my best not to. I never really discussed them. I talked off and on with my first wife about them, but she found that difficult. As a mother, she found it difficult to talk about a child being abused, and she couldn't understand how any parent could treat his or her child the way I was treated. It eventually got to a stage

that whenever I tried to talk about it, it just caused tension and hostility between us.]

The last thing I remember that sunny Thursday afternoon, as I stepped off my deck, was thinking how beautiful the daffodils looked that year. Then it exploded like a cluster bomb in my soul. Instantly, these separate frames or incidents came together like an old 8 mm film, and a movie of my childhood started to play. Memories of sex with my mother, sex with strangers, parties I was taken to, things done to me. I remembered being molested by scout leaders and scout troop members.

I remembered reading my first pornographic magazine at around 5 or 6 years old — *Cavalier* magazine, I believe. I remembered being taken to see *Deep Throat* and *Debbie Does Dallas* by my father at a "Porn and BBQ Night." I remembered being made to stand in front of my mother's feminist support group as they berated me for being a man, and questioned the very need for men to exist at all (I was 11). I remembered being stripped and placed in a circle of my father's friends, ridiculed for my lack of pubic hair and the size of my penis (I was 11). The memories kept coming and coming, one after another — orgies, swinger parties, my father's girlfriends, smells, being confined, scared, paranoid — it didn't stop, and it wouldn't stop for years to come.

That Thursday, my then-wife found me lying on the ground, sobbing uncontrollably, unable to talk, unable to explain. All I could scream was, "THEY FUCKED ME; THEY FUCKED ME, THOSE BASTARDS, THEY FUCKED ME." In that single moment, I had gone from someone struggling to someone incapacitated. As my brain purged itself of these memories I had suppressed

for years, I realized for the first time in my life that I had been sexually abused, and by the experts' definition, "trafficked."

Before that Thursday, I made my living speaking to tens of thousands of people at business events and churches. When I got up off the ground, I had a chronic stutter. Before that Thursday, I used to travel the world. On the following Monday, I couldn't even cope with being stuck in peak-hour traffic in Dallas. I had become deathly afraid of getting lost, getting stuck in an elevator, being touched, or having to talk to strangers — which is a bit bloody hard to do when you're in sales. I had gone from thriving to barely surviving. Over time, I discovered I was suffering from Complex Post-Traumatic Stress Disorder brought on as a result of my childhood environment and years of abuse.

**It never stopped. It just never bloody stopped.**

The memories didn't stop for the next three years. They were relentless, every day, 24 hours a day. Each day there were new details, new memories. I would walk around, and this "movie" would constantly play before me — not in my head, but in front of my eyes, as my mind cleansed itself.

I would be sitting, having lunch in a crowded restaurant with the movie of flashbacks playing. Things I had been a part of and things that had been done to me would constantly be playing before my very eyes. It was a constant, 24/7 nightmare. I remember preaching one day, and all the while my head was continuously playing old porn movies. It was an odd experience, to say the least, and somewhat distracting.

During this period, I trained myself to sleep no more than 90 minutes at a time. I was trying desperately to keep myself out of REM sleep so I wouldn't start to dream and get locked in a nightmare. If I didn't wake-up before the nightmares started, the horror would intensify, and it would take me days to fight my way back to some form of reality.

Unless you have experienced this form of continuous nightmare, it's hard to imagine or explain. Every day I walked around feeling soiled and dirtied by the memories of what was done to me. I had constant visions of sex and pornographic memories. I was exhausted from no sleep. It got so bad that I couldn't tell what was real and what wasn't. I was disoriented and seized by panic attacks.

I didn't know whom to trust. I didn't feel safe anywhere and was scared all the time. I was paranoid someone would hurt my then-wife, children, and me. Smells would trigger memories; movies would trigger memories; a passage in a book or a song would trigger memories — you get the picture. I couldn't escape my head. I was trapped in this hell that wasn't created by me but rather, created *for me.*

I couldn't bear to be separated from my then-wife or kids. Sometimes I followed her to the shopping center to make sure she was safe. I would sit in the car, sobbing, fearful, wait for her to come out of the store, and then quickly drive home so she wouldn't know I had followed her. If I could see her or get her on the phone, then I knew the world would be okay; that I'd be okay; that I could make it through the day and try to get better tomorrow.

I never wanted my kids out of my sight. If I could see them, then I knew no one could hurt them. I didn't want them to stay at friends' places overnight, or go in cars with people I didn't know. If they did, I would be awake and worried all night. I would have to call them to make sure they were safe. If I texted my then-wife or kids and they didn't reply straightaway, my thoughts would get out of control, the voices would start, and I'd get visions of people doing things to them.

My fear led to more arguments with my then-wife. She started to refuse to take my calls, or wait an hour or so before she called me back to teach me not to be controlling. I understand that she was just trying to cope. I understand that overnight the man she married had disappeared and didn't seem to be coming back anytime soon. I get all of that. But it was probably the worst thing she could have done to me at that time. Of course, she didn't know that, and neither did I, and things just got worse for us.

Something happened one particular afternoon that made me realize I was not a well man. I had shutdown my church business and took a job selling above-ground swimming pools to pay the bills. I was in San Antonio on sales calls and pulled into a grocery store to get something for dinner. I picked up a bag of salad, headed to the meat section and was trying to decide between chicken or pork sausages for dinner. I couldn't decide. For some reason, I started to panic about the possibility that I might pick the wrong sausages and wouldn't like them. And only a FUCKING IDIOT WOULD DO SOMETHING LIKE THAT.

I tried to ring my then-wife, but she was with a girlfriend and refused to take my call — she needed "me time." As I stood there, I remembered whom I had been. I used to travel the world, start

and run companies, fly airplanes, scuba dive. I remembered the man I was, and the man I had become wasn't him. The more I screamed at myself, the worse it got.

[ARE YOU SHITTING ME? YOU'RE CRYING OVER BLOODY SAUSAGES. GET YOUR SHIT TOGETHER, MAN. YOU'RE BETTER THAN THIS, BIGGER THAN THIS. HARDEN THE FUCK UP.]

As I stood there, beard covered with snot, sobbing, unable to move, all I could do was pray, "God, please send someone I can trust to help me."

*And the phone rang.*

### The *Parable of the Foolish Man*

A gatekeeper was responsible for the gate to a small town. One day a man came to the gate and asked, "What kind of town is this?" The gatekeeper replied, "From what kind of town did you come?" The newcomer's report was one of dissatisfaction, disharmony, and disgust. The gatekeeper replied: "You will find this town to be the same." The man went on somewhere else.

The next day, another man came and inquired of the little town. The gatekeeper again asked, "From what kind of town did you come? The man gave a glowing report of his former home speaking of the love, the sharing, and the goodwill which characterized the inhabitants. To this, the gatekeeper replied, "Come in! This place will be to you just as that from which you come!"

—James Oppenheim

## RE-DEFINING NORMAL

When I got back from that trip to San Antonio, I accepted that I would never be *normal* again.

The conversation I had with myself went something like this:

*"Are you kidding me? WTF! Dude, you got issues, just buy both sausages next time!*

*Did you see the look on the store clerk's face? You're a 6-foot, 230-pound man, all inked up with a shaved head, crying over FUCKING SAUSAGES. YOU NEARLY GOT TAZED.*

*You are never going to be normal again, get it ... NEVER ... Just accept it. That whole sausage deal was bullshit. You've got to get your shit together.*

*Anyway, what the hell is normal? Why is that so important? If you really want to be normal, you are going to have to re-define that for yourself."*

I was trying so hard to be normal for everyone on the outside. On the inside, day after day, I was utterly out of control. The smallest sounds, smells, conversations or movies would trigger new memories that would flood my mind and leave me swearing and crying for hours. These outbursts were inflicted on everyone around me. They washed over me for days; followed by days of regret and recrimination with what I had said. I remember apologizing, yet again, to my then-wife. Her response was, "I know you're sorry, but that doesn't make it easier, and it doesn't mean it won't happen again. You can't change."

She was right. It would happen again and again and again; that is the nature of C-PTSD. I knew at that point that my marriage was screwed.

Normal for me was panic and paranoia.

Distrust and dislike.

Depression and hopelessness.

Normal people don't have to try to be *normal*, they just are.

So I raged.

I raged in anger, fear, and regret; but mostly frustration at my inability to beat the consequences of someone else's selfish and sick actions. There was no relief; nothing I tried seemed to work, and I was afraid it would never stop.

If I had cancer, it would have been easier for my loved ones. They would have had something they could understand, something they could get their minds around. My then-wife would have received support. The kids would have been able to say, "My dad's got cancer," instead of not talking about how *Daddy sometimes has bad days because when he was 13 he got a head job from his scout master, he dreamt about it again, and woke up screaming and crying hysterically.*

I would sit in my shed, hopeless, and helpless. Crying away the days and dreading the nights. These memories broke me. They broke me in hard places; in places that could never be seen; and in places that could not be easily accessed. I didn't know what to do or how to fix it. My then-wife couldn't cope. She couldn't understand why God allowed me to marry her and why He allowed these things to happen to me as a child. She came to believe I was the worst thing that ever happened to her. I had to agree, at the time, I probably was. I was a challenge to live with, but what could I do? I was fighting for my very survival. I know now that back then I was a very distressed and sick man.

On two occasions, I nursed a gun and a bottle, planning a way to end my pain. This wasn't an emotional process. It was a very calm conclusion I arrived at because I was the cause of great suffering and distress. I wasn't trying to stop my pain; I knew I could learn to live with that. I needed to stop the pain I was inflicting on my family.

What stopped me? On both occasions, the phone rang.

*Another phone call.*

As the years went on, I started to fill what I later called my "toolbox" (see the Appendix on p. 335) with the emotional and social tools I needed to cope with everyday life. Unfortunately for my marriage, the years of sickness, conflict, and stress proved to be too much. I ended up divorced and estranged from my kids. My ability to make an income dwindled to nothing.

I had just turned 50, and in essence, I had lost it all. I was living in a single bedroom apartment with a mattress on the floor. It was too small for the kids to stay over. I bought some camping cots for the lounge room, but they sucked. My kids were embarrassed and ashamed of their dad and hurt by the divorce. I felt like all I needed were boils, and I would have given Job from The Old-Testament a run for his money.

I only had one option open to me. It was time for me to pick up the broken pieces of my life and go again — I was just going to have to *deal with it* all.

I started writing poetry and publishing it online anonymously. It was part of my process — my search for meaning and healing. I thought that if all this happened to me, then there must be other men out there who also experienced something similar. Maybe my writing could help them?

One morning, I was sitting on my little balcony in my crappy apartment complex, reading my Bible, listening to Martin Lloyd-Jones, and smoking a cigar for breakfast. I was listening to the

people next door fighting because they hadn't had sex for a month (lucky bastards ... only a month) while watching old Mrs. Patterson run away from Buster, the beagle. Buster had gotten out again and was trying to hump her leg as she scrambled away on her walking frame.

*The phone rang.* It was Melissa, and she was using her emphatic voice.

"John, have you looked at your email?"

I smiled as I imagined her waving her arms around while trying to drive, hold the phone and balance a cup of coffee. *"No, I am watching Ethel try to get away from Buster. Buster is winning."*

"You need to read it. No, don't read it. Okay, read it, but the answer's no; you shouldn't do it. No way. It's a horrible idea. I am coming over right now, and I'll help you draft an email response that says no. I'm from South Carolina, and we are trained from birth to say no in such a way that people thank you for it."

I sat there for a while, deciding whether to help Ethel or let Buster have his jollies. I picked up a tennis ball, hit Buster in the back of the head, fist-pumped my own awesomeness, and went to check my email.

There was a group out of Bonham, Texas, a bunch of Jain nuns and monks that had read my poetry on Twitter, and it seemed like I was a bit of a unicorn to them. I was the only male survivor that seemed willing to speak about what happened to him as a kid, and they wanted to know if I would be interviewed on camera for a documentary on human trafficking.

It took 20 minutes for Mel to get there. She walked in talking passionately about my mental health. I was right, the empathic hands were waving, so I knew she was serious. She was talking about how this was the worst thing I could do for my mental and emotional health. How there must be other people out there who could help them and that I didn't need to worry about it, the monks would find someone else, and now that we had resolved that — would I like some real breakfast?

I very calmly and slowly said, *"I'm doing it. If I don't do this now, then I never will."*

"But you're not ready for it. You're not well enough yet."

I said, *"I never will be. I have learned that at the times that I am least prepared, when I least feel like I can, or when I am fearful of something, those are the times I need to not think something through, but run at it."*

"But it will bring all the memories back. It does every time you talk about it; you will be sick for days," she said.

*"I know, but what if my kids saw it? Or my ex-wife? Maybe someday they will understand that I wasn't trying to be an arsehole, that I was just sick. Maybe they will believe that what happened to me was true and that PTSD is a real thing and not SOME BULLSHIT I MADE UP BECAUSE I WAS A FUCKING ARSEHOLE WHO HATED THEM AND WAS TOO WEAK AND TOO FUCKING STUPID AND TOO MUCH OF A FUCKING CHILD TO CONTROL MYSELF."*

She stood there quietly while I raged on for about 20 minutes. I raged against the world, my parents, my mind, and Buster's owners because every day Ethel was scared, and the people downstairs for fighting about sex instead of shagging like rabbits. Screamed that I wasn't a manipulator or a child; I was just fucked up, and I needed it all to stop and to mean something. I told her I never blamed God, but I prayed every day that He would do something good with it all. Maybe this would be the good.

Then, all the memories started to flood back, and I was once again 13 in a tent, with my scout leader playing with my dick, telling me this is what real men do to each other, while the other boys watched and waited their turn.

I sat there crying, totally overwhelmed by my feelings of vulnerability, failure, guilt, fear, and paranoia.

Then slowly Mel started to talk to me like before when I had an episode. I could hear her, softly reassuring me, that voice on the end of the phone when I needed it most. I told myself, "You can trust her, slow down, listen, it will be okay, she won't hurt you."

She said, "John, look at me, do you see me? Come back; it's okay. I see you. Do you hear me? I hear you; I am standing right in front of you. Take my hand. Do you feel my hand; that is real. I am real. You're safe now."

*[I hate them. Look what they did to me. I am a fucking spastic stuck in a fucking shitty apartment; my life is shit. I can't talk normally; I can't go outside, I cry all day ... LOOK WHAT THOSE ARSEHOLES DID TO ME. SOMEONE HAS TO STAND UP TO THEM. NO ONE STOOD UP FOR ME.]*

She waited while I cried and screamed some more, then cupped my face and said, "I see you, I hear you. If you need to do this, then we will do this together. I'll help you. I'll be right there beside you. How about next week? Why don't we ask them to shoot the video here in the apartment, so you feel safe? Maybe on Wednesday?"

*"I only have one chair."*

"I'll give you my chairs."

*"They will probably only include a small part of it anyway. They will probably film lots of other people."*

"They might not use any of it. That would be okay, wouldn't it?"

*"Sure, that would be fine. I don't need to be in there; I just need to not be scared of people knowing anymore. I don't want to be scared ANYMORE, MEL. I WANT IT ALL TO STOP."*

"It's okay. Why don't you go have a lie-down, and I'll draft an email."

*"Okay."*

It was dark when I woke, and Mel had gone, but the smell of her and the dinner she made me filled my apartment; and I knew it would be okay.

# NORMAL

Neutral

Ordinary

Routine

Mundane

Average

Listless

Taken from *No Working Title: a Life in Progress* by Dr. John A. King, available at www.drjohnaking.com.

**NOW WHAT?**

As I said before, I could no longer live up to normal with my then-wife. I just couldn't. What the hell was happy and normal anyway? I had no idea. I thought I was happy and normal before John-A-Geddon (as my internal marketing department called it).

So, I decided to re-define normal for myself and somehow work out what it meant to be happy again. Why? Because to be honest folks, I was bloody miserable and there was nothing normal about me anymore.

In my attempts to be normal for everyone, I followed a rigorous daily routine. I had to have all my ducks lined up in a row. If I didn't, I'd end up in a heap, crying, or in a rage, screaming about sausages.

Every day, I attempted to maintain a strict routine to minimize triggering flashbacks of memories and thereby, an episode.

My new routine included:

- Bed by 8 P.M. in an attempt to get some sleep before the nightmares started.
- Wake up before 2 A.M. because the worst dreams seem to come around then.
- Read for an hour; lie down again around 3 A.M.
- Try to sleep until 4:30 A.M.; get up and be at the gym by 5 A.M.
- Train until 7 A.M.
- Come home and have breakfast with the kids.
- Read my Bible and a book.

- Start prep on three sermons between 9 A.M. and Noon.
- Schedule business meetings from Noon until dinner.

I would have to be very careful about what I ate and did:

- No sugar because it brought on anxiety and depression.
- Very selective with movies and music because it brought back bad memories.
- No scented detergents or fragrances because they might induce flashbacks.
- Not being in crowds or surrounded by too many people for too long, or I would become incredibly fearful, and a panic attack would start.
- Not being touched without warning, or I would violently and fearfully recoil. It was even painful to touch my kids; for some reason it felt like broken glass. And yet, I was desperate for sexual and intimate touch with my then-wife. I needed to be held by her, told I was safe, and that she would never leave me. But every day she drifted away from me, unable to cope with what I was going through, and angry with God for being married to me. We stopped having sex.
- No loud noises or loud music.
- Taking 20 to 30 vitamins and/or supplements a day to improve cognition and sleep.
- Injecting myself with supplements two or three times a week because my pituitary gland had been non-functioning for so long that my endocrine system was nearly shut down.
- Sitting for hours in my shed – writing and rewriting poetry in an attempt to tame the rage; along with and processing all I was recalling and dealing with.

This regimen was all in an effort to live a normal life for everyone around me, so they might hopefully, see me trying and not give up on me.

Then one day, at the point of exhaustion, at 3 o'clock in the afternoon, I fell asleep in my office during a staff meeting. I woke an hour later incredibly embarrassed, but felt near superhuman, like I could do anything. I was so energized. For the next two weeks, I locked my office door; told folks I was on a call and slept. I felt incredibly guilty because normal people didn't take naps at 3 o'clock in the afternoon.

Soon after all this started, I had a simple thought — my childhood wasn't normal when compared to everybody else, so maybe my adulthood wouldn't have to be *normal* compared to theirs either? What the hell is *normal* anyway?

The definition of *normal* provided to me by others in my life was habitual, expected, accustomed.

I decided that instead of living up to someone else's standard and definition of what my day-to-day life should be like, I gave myself permission to re-define my normal.

I looked at my life and asked the simple questions: *"What was normal for me? Who was I? What did a normal day look like for me?"*

You see, I felt like two men. In a sense, I didn't recognize myself anymore. I saw my reflection in the mirror, but didn't feel the same, think the same, or want the same things I wanted before. I found out years later that that's exactly what happened because my

brain indeed actually had changed. The memories, the emotions, the anxiety all played a role in fundamentally changing the way my neurological pathways behaved, which changed my skills, abilities, and even desires.

I was watching Fight Club one night and a particular statement by Tyler Durden struck me:

> "I see in Fight Club the strongest and smartest men who've ever lived. I see all this potential, and I see squandering. God damn it, an entire generation pumping gas, waiting tables; slaves with white collars. Advertising has us chasing cars and clothes, working jobs we hate so we can buy shit we don't need. We're the middle children of history, man. No purpose or place. We have no Great War. No Great Depression. Our Great War's a spiritual war; our Great Depression is our lives. We've all been raised on television to believe that one day we'd all become millionaires, and movie gods, and rock stars. But we won't. And we're slowly learning that fact. And we're very, very pissed off."

I looked around at people I once thought were *normal*, and the vast majority seemed to be going through life in a daze. They were buying things they didn't want, with money they didn't have, to impress people they didn't like, and working three jobs to pay for it all. They spent so much effort trying to be perfect or trying to be happy that they couldn't stop long enough and just BE.

It seemed that they were all too busy to BE anything, let alone content. No one appeared to be moving at a pace where you could enjoy anything in life, let alone take a nap if you needed one. I

wondered ... *just wondered* ... if what happened to me wasn't the worst thing to ever happen in my life, but maybe the best? Maybe somewhere in all of this mess was something of beauty and value that I had yet to discover?

So I rewrote my *normal* in a positive, purposeful manner:

- I get up at 2 A.M. some mornings, so having a nap at 3 P.M. is a very normal thing to do. I do it because my body needs the sleep, not because I am ill.
- I'm an athlete and a body builder; this is why I go to the gym.
- I enjoy being physically fit and eating healthy all the time.
- I don't eat sugar, and I take supplements because it's good for my health.
- I'm not a recluse; I just enjoy time by myself to enjoy the life I have.
- I'm not depressed; I'm a poet and a writer. I go to bed early, so I can rise early and pursue my art.
- I don't go out in crowds because I like to be at home with people I love and who love me.

From that moment on, I started to enjoy life and began to accept who I was. I began to get a sense that there might even be a future out there waiting for me. I started to forgive myself for a failed marriage and estranged kids. I forgave myself for the collapse of the church and having to shut down the business. I started to accept that these were doors closing, and I was simply waiting for new ones to open.

I came to understand that it wasn't so much a matter of re-defining normal as it was in accepting my new Self and what was normal for me. I had to stop being harsh and critical. I needed

to celebrate my resilience and my ability to survive and prosper for so many years when others did not. I had to start to embrace the new me and to see my new needs, passions and desires, not as restrictions, but as life choices. If I could do that, then maybe life wasn't over for me?

Maybe I would even find someone to share it all with? Maybe I wouldn't die a "miserable, pathetic, unloved man" as I was told I would? Maybe someone, somewhere would love me, could love me? Maybe when I got my shit together-ish, I would find someone? But I didn't need to focus on that now.

Sure, Mel was around, but she was like that - the type of person who rescues dogs, horses, and old furniture. I just figured she'd move on, like everyone else, because she knew all my crap and eventually it would become too much for her. I'd be too much for her, and she would move on. They all moved on eventually. I got it. I was fucked up. I was hard to live with, but that was okay. I just somehow knew it would all be okay.

## MEL'S TURN

When I read the email from the nuns, my gut reaction was, "NO, DEFINITELY NOT ... bad idea!" Because every time John told his story, spoke about or shared it, it was hard on him. Okay, not just hard — *crippling*.

And so here he was, going through a divorce — which makes even the sanest person crazy, and he wants to recount his story — you do the math. Not just for a couple of monkish people he's never met, but on camera, for the world to see.

To be honest, it's exactly the way John does things. He's just not a toes-in-the-water-to-check-the-temperature sort of guy ... he's more of a jump-in-head-first-and-curse-loudly-when-you-get-a-shock sort of guy. So what could I do but go along? Who am I to tell him what his process for recovery should be?

My process, as a toes-in-the-water individual, is to consider the possibilities. And I had. At least 20 minutes of every worst-case scenario I could conjure, as I drove to his apartment that day. And then at least an hour or so more, as he went to bed, exhausted at even the thought of being on camera.

Up until that point, he had published his poetry (and his story) online, anonymously. Clearly, anonymity was SO 2015 (dripping with sarcasm). I could see it was time to move on to bravery, transparency ... who knew what else the future might hold?

So when Mr. Jump-in-head-first says, "Oh crap, what have I done?" I know the best answer is often none at all.

I never knew how important or timely my phone calls were until John started writing this book. We just worked together back then, so he never told me. I only knew a fraction of what he was going through.

You know all those times when someone crosses your mind and you think, "Oh, I should call that person?" Well, don't wait. Pick up the phone. It might be a really important call. Or maybe you're the one going through something — reach out. I know it takes incredible bravery. If all you can do is send a text, do that. None of us are meant to do life alone. We all need help choosing sausages sometimes.

One thing about this time in John's life, the sort of rock-bottom-living-in-a-one-room-flat days, is that he never asked, "Why me?" or "How could God let something like this happen?"

John actually never blamed God at all. His faith in God did not waver, even when his faith in himself was shattered. All he ever asked in prayer was that God would turn everything that happened to him around for good.

John's certainly not a perfect man, and he'll be the first to tell you that he's difficult to live with some days. Don't ever think we're trying to say everything is fun or funny or rosy. We laugh A LOT and make fun of ourselves A LOT because we have to. It's way better than crying. We take the difficulties as they come and learn as much from them as we can.

John still has nightmares. He talks and cries and fights in his sleep — all night sometimes. Sometimes he wakes up really mad at me for something I did in his dreams. He still gets exhausted

some days and has to lie down, particularly if he gets drained emotionally. But he gets up and TRIES HARD every single day. What more could I ask of him?

## CHAPTER TWO

# Never a Victim

I am many things:

Imperfect, a work in progress, a man trying to own his crap,

But I have never been a victim, be it of sexual abuse or anything else.

A victim has already lost their battle; I have just begun to fight.

—Dr. John A. King, *No Working Title*

**Me:** *Here is my life story.*
**Therapist:** *(Burst into tears after first session) That's the worst case I have ever heard of; I can't help you, it's too much for me.*
**Me:** *WTF?!*

You should know that I've never been comfortable with the term victim. I only once called myself a victim and that was right at the beginning of things. When it all came together for me and played like an old movie – when that happened for the first time – that was the only time I called myself a *victim of abuse*. My then-wife said that any of the *frames* or stories I told her about were horrible abuse, but I never saw it like that. For me, it was just my life; the only life I'd ever known.

But the day the memories and flashbacks all came together changed everything for me. As I lay there sobbing, the person I cried for wasn't me the man, but the boy I had been. In the months after the recall, I didn't see my now-Self as a victim, and I didn't even see my then-Self as a victim. I just wept for what happened to a little boy who had no way to protect himself and no way to fight back.

I think it's that sense of injustice that has driven me my whole life. I look back at the fights I had in school and the arguments I had as an adult and recognize that I don't like bullies. I don't like those who use their power, status, or stature to humiliate or take from someone who is defenseless.

Even though I didn't see myself as a victim, I knew I was a mess. I had exhausted my limits of knowledge and tenacity, and I didn't see progress. I needed to find a support group. I searched around the Dallas/Fort Worth area to discover the only support groups available were for women and that men were not welcomed there. I called rape groups, but apparently, men don't get raped. I remember calling a church recovery group, and the receptionist told me I was a pervert just trying to have sex with broken women. I told her to "fuck off."

Obviously, a support group wasn't going to work; so, I thought, *"How about a therapist?"*

A guy I was doing business with at the time, knew a little of my story and suggested if I ever wanted to speak to someone, his mother-in-law Mona was an excellent choice. He told me Mona had a difficult childhood and has spent 30 years or so dealing with abuse cases of the worst kind; so, she wasn't new to the field, but she lived in South Dakota. I thought, *"Awesome, I can tell her my crap and never see her again!"*

My time with Mona was exceptional and essential for my progress on my journey at the time; but it sure did start off shaky.

Day 1 - Enter the Dragon.

I was supposed to be in South Dakota for three weeks in November 2013 to finish up some prep for a body-building competition. I was in the throes of all the typical Post-Traumatic Stress Disorder symptoms at the time: paranoia, fear, flight, and anxiety. I struggled daily to establish what was real and whom I could trust. Yet, I knew if I were going to move forward, I needed help. I had gotten about as far as I could with books. I called Mona's office and arranged for our first exploratory session.

Now let me be very clear here, the thought of going in and chatting with some strange woman about all my crap was about as comfortable as riding a bronco on a barbwire saddle - painful in a very intimate way.

Sioux Falls is a beautiful city and in November it's like a winter wonderland. I arrived at Mona's office about 45 minutes early.

The soft white virginal snowflakes drifted serenely and fluffily to the ground. It was a perfect Hallmark moment, pierced only by the sound of me dry heaving with fear behind the car, which went like this:

*"Whose stupid idea was this anyway?! What the hell was I thinking? (heave)*

*I am about to go in that building over there, and I am going to sit down and talk to some bloody woman about all this shit in my life. (heave)*

*She is probably going to say I have to be honest with her; then I am going to have to talk about having things shoved up my arse. (heave)*

*I'll give you shoved up the arse you; you made this bloody appointment, what a stupid idea. (heave)*

*I am out of here."*

Instead of putting the car in drive, I put it in reverse, mashed the pedal and ran into a snow bank. Then opened the door and heaved.

I had just shut the door and was cleaning my beard of bagel chunks when the smallest, meekest grandma-type person in the world came over and tapped on the window and screamed, "I AM SATAN, AND I AM GOING TO RIP YOUR SOUL OUT OF YOUR BODY AND POST YOUR PATHETIC STORY ON FACEBOOK."

Well, that's what I thought she said. She probably said something more like, "Are you John?"(heave)

**Me:** "Yes, hi, I'm John, funny thing, the car just jumped in reverse."

**Devil woman:** "Yes, that seems to happen quite a lot on first visits. Why don't you just leave it there for now, and we will get a tow truck after your session?"

Bitch, she was on to me. I was stuck. I climbed out of the car, slipped on my arse and followed Mrs. Diablo into her office, waddling like a duck with soaked track pants.

She handed me a clipboard that only asked for name, address, etc. She apparently only took payment in cash, not the soul of my first-born. I didn't see any pentagrams sprayed over her Thomas Kinkade. This Diablo was good, but I wasn't convinced. We went back to her nice little office that mockingly overlooked the car park and the site of my not-so-successful escape attempt.

She gave me a little moment to get settled and offered me a therapist mint; you know, the ones that are laced with truth serum that say *lifesaver* on the side — it's all subliminal, friend.

She asked, "Why South Dakota and why me? I'm sure there are therapists in Texas we could find for you?"

"Well," I said, "I know your son-in-law, and he says you can be trusted. I don't trust easily anymore, maybe I never have. But I know that I have come as far as I can come on my journey alone. I've read all I know to read. I need help. I need tools if I am ever going to have a chance to get beyond this point in my life. The fact is, I am stuck, and I hate being stuck."

She gave me that practiced therapist smile and leaned back in her slightly reclining therapist desk chair and said, "We have about 30 minutes, why don't you tell me your story, and we will make a plan together?"

I remember sitting there with wet palms and shaking hands, knowing I had to make a decision:

> 1). I could yell fuck off and jump out the window, but the back two tires of my car were 18" off the ground.
> 2). I could bullshit her and get out of there in 30 minutes and never come back - who needs this shit anyway?
> 3). I could tell the woman the truth - all of it. I could take a chance one more time and maybe she could help.

So I started.

"My earliest memory is my father putting bread and water... "

At 30 minutes the buzzer went off, and I stopped mid-sentence and looked at her. She was sitting there with her head slightly down. She just nodded and said, "Keep going, let's make time."

Again at 60 minutes, she said, "Let me call Nancy and move an appointment. Now explain that to me again, they did what to you with pliers?"

After 90 minutes, I stopped, reached for a jar of M&M's she had there for small children and started to pick out the yellow ones.

It was done. I was done. I told Mona everything; every last detail of everything I had recalled so far.

She slowly raised her head, looked at me, burst into tears and said, "That is the most horrible thing I have ever heard in my professional career."

With my hand stuck in the jar, I said, "I'm sorry, what did you say?"

"That is the worst story I have heard in 30 years of counseling. I am sorry John, that's too much, way too much, for me. I would never be able to help you; I don't have the skills or the experience to help you. I don't have the answers. I am so very, very sorry for your pain, John, that's just terrible. Your life has been terrible."

I sat there and thought, *"I'm screwed. I am totally and utterly screwed. I'm fucked. I mean not just a little bit, but all the way, completely fucked. I mean, I am fucked, and then fucked some more. WTF."*

And we sat there. Mona sobbing quietly; me trying to get my hand out of the jar.

Finally, when she had settled down, and I worked out that if I opened my hand I could get out the last yellow M&M, I said, "No, I'm sorry Mona, that's not how this works out. I didn't come here looking for you to be my savior; I came looking for someone to help me gather some tools for my next stage of recovery. I don't need you to know everything; I just need you to know more than I do at this point in my life. I just need you to be trustworthy. I just need you to be honest with me. I'll take care of the rest."

We sat a little longer, and she said: "I'm sorry John, that was very unprofessional of me, I have never broken down like that, it's just so hard for me to hear a story like that."

"You should try living the story; it's worse," I said.

We laughed a little. At that point, the horns receded and all that was left was grey hair, and I said, "I've chosen you, Mona, I've decided to trust you. If it is not you, then I will never do a therapist again. I know that is a big statement, but I also know me. I am not trying to manipulate anything; I am just telling the truth. I don't have the internal fortitude to do this again; it hurts too much."

She told me she was going to call her mentor to discuss it, and we would chat tomorrow.

Day 2 - Round 2.

The next day I ate, hit the gym, ate, did cardio, ate, and went to see Mona.

"I spoke to my mentor, and he said he has never heard a story like yours either."

On a scale of 1 to 10, I went from perfectly calm to about 1000. I was about to go postal.

"But (I love that word)," she said, "I can help you. I don't know how much, but I believe I can give you some more - how did you say it - tools for your toolbox, I like that." (See the Appendix on p. 337 for the toolbox)

I cried. I had trusted someone. I took a chance. It was going to work out.

She took my hand and said, "I can see you once a week for six months and that should get you going, how does that work?"

I smiled my best smile and said, "We can't do it that way, Mona. I need to see you every day. I am only here for three weeks. In fact, I think I should see you twice a day for the next three weeks. That will be about the same as six months' worth of visits."

"That is impossible, John. No one can do that much therapy; it is too intense. No one can handle that much processing."

I just looked at her and waited.

She shook her head and laughed, and we compromised. (Thank God for that. If she had called my bluff, I would have been screwed. Twice a day, every day, are you kidding me, I might be crazy, but I'm not stupid!)

So we set our calendars - Tuesday, Thursday, and Friday.

I would eat, train, do therapy, eat, sleep, do therapy, do cardio, eat, sleep. The off days, I would eat, train, write, sleep, train, eat, sleep.

It was a total beating. I was beyond tired. I was beyond drained. I would cry for days at a time. I burst into tears on the cardio equipment at the gym or sitting over lunch. It was winter and my tears and snot would freeze in my beard as I walked back to the hotel. But I was happy, so stinking happy. I now had hope. I not only had identified an opponent - my dreams, my past, my memories - I had a ring to fight them in: my therapy sessions with my very own grey-haired Mickey Goldmill in my corner.

In our third meeting, Mona gave me the greatest gift she could ever have given me. Something I never had before. As we wrapped the session up, she looked at me and shook her cute little grey head and laughed, saying, "John, you are the most resilient person I have ever known. There is no way you could have survived what you have been through and remained as whole as you are if you weren't."

I had never seen myself as a victim, but up until that point, I didn't have any other way to describe myself. Now I did. I could say to myself, *"I am resilient."*

When she looked at me, she didn't see the mess-ups, the screw-ups, or the broken pieces. She looked at me and saw ME. She saw through the anger, the rage, the story, the past, and she SAW ME.

On the dark days going forward, and there have been thousands, I would never again call myself broken. I would never even call myself a survivor; I was more than any of that, I was RESILIENT.

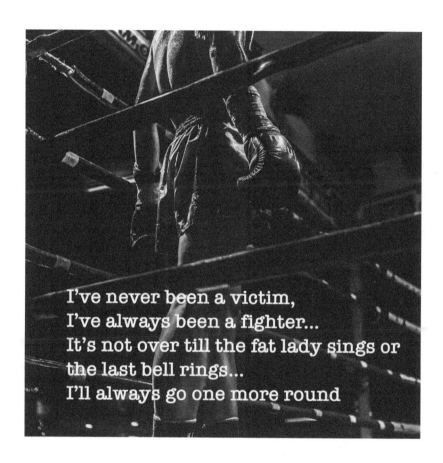

Meme created by Dr. John A. King, originally published at drjohnaking.com.
Photo by Ryan Tang on unsplash.com

## YOU MIGHT BE RIGHT, I MIGHT BE CRAZY

I believe that whatever doesn't kill you simply makes you stranger.

—The Joker, *The Dark Knight*

'Cuz in this life,
Things are much harder than in the afterworld.
In this life,
You're on your own.
And if the elevator tries to bring you down,
Go crazy - punch a higher floor.

—Prince, *Let's Go Crazy*

Four thoughts before we have a chat about being crazy:

**Thought #1:** *There are three kinds of lies: lies, damned lies, and statistics.*

I know this will put some people into a world-class personal agenda meltdown, but your reaction exposes your agenda. Mine is apparent, has often been stated and has never wavered: sexual abuse and human trafficking are human rights' issues, not gender rights' issues.

Summar Ghias, the program specialist for the Chicago-based International Organization for Adolescents, said: "We're conditioned as a community to identify female victims more

readily, because that has been the more prominent focus of the anti-trafficking movement."[1]

The stats that are reported on sexual abuse and trafficking of boys and men are somewhere between 15%-25%. However, these numbers *massively under-represent* the worldwide tragedy. Get anywhere outside of first-world countries, and the number of boys and men abused and trafficked are higher overall than the number of girls and women abused or trafficked. In first-world countries, the reported percentage of boys and men abused or trafficked seems to sit between 40%-60% of the population, depending on the study.[2]

The incredibly needed and helpful dialogue, government and community resourcing, and public support that women and girls receive, has yet to make it to the male population. When asked why government and police organizations in New York seemed to have a bias in their views toward boys, with not allocating resources to help them get out of trafficking situations, Genna Goldsobel, state policy coordinator of ECPAT-USA said, "How

---

1 http://jjie.org/2014/04/14/trafficked-boys-overlooked-underrepresented/106688/

2 http://www.givethemavoice.foundation/the-voice/men-boys-represent-half-trafficked/

http://www.givethemavoice.foundation/the-voice/men-boys-perilous-situation/

http://www.givethemavoice.foundation/the-voice/concern-abuse-men-forgotten-gender/

http://www.givethemavoice.foundation/the-voice/52-9-boys-sexual-abused/

http://www.givethemavoice.foundation/the-voice/boys-left-out-in-the-fight-against-human-trafficking-and-sexual-abuse/

can a boy be trafficked; they're much stronger than girls, they could get out of it if they wanted to do so."[3]

A Juvenile Justice Information Report stated:[4]

"Experts say that the law enforcement's attitudes toward male victims are still weighed down by gender biases in trafficking discourse, which pins females as victims and males as perpetrators. Therefore, male victims in custody often fall through the cracks of services that could be offered to help them because they are not properly assessed for sexual exploitation."

The report went to say:

"Victims are unwilling to come forward to service providers, which may include doctors, social workers, and probation officers, due to feelings of shame and stigma."

**Thought #2:** *My dirty little secret.*

People ask me why so few men talk about their sexual abuse. If the research shows that the number of boys abused is closer to 50%, yet the reported cases seem to consistently come in at around 20%, why the disparity? Well, men don't talk about what they've experienced because it's not the sort of conversation they've given themselves permission to have yet; nor is it the

---

3 http://jjie.org/2014/04/14/trafficked-boys-overlooked-underrepresented/106688/

4 http://jjie.org/2014/04/14/trafficked-boys-overlooked-underrepresented/106688/

sort of conversation that society is comfortable to allow them to hold. Here is some feedback I received from men over the years:

*"A real man isn't a victim of anything. Asking for help is a sign of weakness. I don't want to sit down and talk about my feelings; we need to be strong."*

*"I tried to once, but the woman said that men couldn't get raped."*

*"When he touched me, I got hard, so I thought I must like it, maybe I was gay. I'm not, but that is what I struggled with."*

*"My friends thought it was awesome that my aunty wanted to blow me, so I didn't talk to anyone about how it made me feel, I wanted to be cool at school. I didn't think it was abuse till I got married and it started to cause us some issues."*

**Thought #3**: *I'm friends with the monster.*[5]

If you break your leg, the ladies at church bring you chicken potpie. If you lose your legs, people give you understanding and compassion, and they tend to speak to your greatness, not your limitation. If you have a mental illness, you're lumped in with the same group of killers from the Columbine or the Oklahoma bombing - you're considered unstable, unemployable, and they look at you like you're probably going to start randomly slaughtering people at any moment.

On more than one occasion, by those closest to me at the time of my recall, I was called crazy, lazy, a coward, and a fraud - often

---

5 *Monster* by Eminem

all in the same argument. What they couldn't see or understand scared them. People cannot see mental illness, and they don't take the time to understand it.

My whole childhood, I was called stupid, thick, dense, Captain Concrete, shit-for-brains. The list of non-creative insults was never ending. It was a game Fred[6] (my father) encouraged his friends to participate in when I did something he didn't like.

I remember working on a car with Fred and some of his friends once. I made a mistake, and they all stood around and started the name-calling. That was when I was made to drop my pants and was called a girl because I hadn't fully developed. I think I was about 11 years old; that was a tough year (I also lost my dog).

The one name I was called, both at school and after John-A-Geddon, which hurt me the most was *retard*.

In Australia, high school goes from 12 to 18 years of age. In my first year, I remember being out on the school rugby field with a short redheaded freckle-faced kid. The older boys, the jocks (as called in America) decided they wanted the field. We were getting out of the way and everything was going fine until they called my mate a redheaded retard. What happened next I can't remember. All I know is that I was dragged off the school bully by a teacher and two of his friends. It was a little bit like the basement scene in Fight Club.

---

6 Not a real name. I refer to them as Fred and Rosemary going forward, after Fred and Rosemary West.

**Thought #4:** *And the winner is... STIGMA*

All three (Thoughts 1, 2 and 3) share the commonality of an incredible social stigma attached to them. If you're a man who has been abused or trafficked as a child and later on in life you end up suffering from the onset of a mental illness, the likelihood of you being willing, resourced, or even able to seek help for your situation is very low.

So not only are you screwed up, crazy, and abandoned, there is no one to help you.

Here are two definitions of stigma, according to dictionary.com:

1). A mark of disgrace or infamy; a stain or reproach; and
2). A mental or physical mark that is characteristic of a defect or disease.

For survivors of abuse, it feels like that. We are entirely sure that people can see the stain of the past. Every look is a sneer; every relationship is simply a chance to get rejected and used again. With PTSD, it's more complicated. You can isolate yourself; become paranoid; are sometimes anxious in big rooms with no people or in small rooms with many people; Can be comfortable around strangers or wholly uncomfortable around strangers. And half the time you're convinced they're reading your mind and know your past. So you pretend, you put on the show and don't let people emotionally or physically close enough to hurt you.

Capital Letter Syndrome

On two separate occasions in August 1943, General George S. Patton slapped and berated two U.S. Army soldiers after discovering that, though they had no apparent physical injuries, they had been evacuated to hospitals far away from the front lines. They were suffering *shell shock* and were considered cowards. That is what Patton called them. Nowadays we understand that battle-weary veterans aren't cowards, but suffer from a mental disorder that is the result of extended exposure to traumatic events.

Advancement in military science and technology always ends up filtering into our everyday life; for example, duct tape, microwave ovens, and GPS. It's the same with our understanding of the impact of trauma on the human mind.

Before U.S. military efforts, Austrian physician Josef Leopold (1761) wrote about "nostalgia" among soldiers. Among those exposed to military trauma, some reported missing home, feeling sad, sleeping problems, and anxiety. This description of PTSD-like symptoms was one model of psychological injury that existed into the Civil War.

A second model of this condition suggested a physical injury as the cause of symptoms. "Soldier's heart" or "irritable heart" was marked by a rapid pulse, anxiety, and trouble breathing. U.S. doctor Jacob Mendez Da Costa studied Civil War soldiers with these cardiac symptoms and described them as over stimulation

of the heart's nervous system, or *Da Costa's Syndrome*. Soldiers often returned to battle after receiving drugs to control symptoms.[7]

Usually, people who have suffered trauma have received the common diagnosis from their exes as arsehole and jerk. Therapists/psychiatrists tend to be a little more professional and occasionally more compassionate. The standard classifications we receive are Personality Disorder (PD), Borderline Personality Disorder (BPD), Post Traumatic Stress (PTS), Post Traumatic Stress Disorder (PTSD), or Complex-Post Traumatic Stress Disorder (C-PTSD). I know, lots of letters. They all look the same - massively confusing and somewhat intimidating. I want to give you a quick and straightforward rundown of the different meanings, along with a brief description:

- Personality Disorder (PD)is pervasive and affects someone on a daily basis.[8]

- Borderline Personality Disorder (BPD) is characterized by particular patterns of emotionally driven behavior, including instability of interpersonal relationships, impulse control, and self-image. This results in impairments in self-management and the achievement of goals, as well as deficits in social interactions.[9]

- Post Traumatic Stress (PTS) is a standard response to experiencing a traumatic or stressful event like a car accident, a job loss, or a house fire.[10] The effects of PTS

---

7 https://www.ptsd.va.gov/public/PTSD-overview/basics/history-of-ptsd-vets.asp

8 http://www.ptsduk.org/what-is-ptsd/

9 http://www.borderline-personality-disorder.com

10 https://www.brainline.org/article/what-are-differences-between-pts-and-ptsd

are short-term, usually only lasting weeks, or at the most a month or two.

- Post Traumatic Stress Disorder (PTSD) is a condition that's triggered by a terrifying event or events, either from experiencing it or witnessing it. Symptoms may include flashbacks, nightmares and severe anxiety, as well as uncontrollable thoughts about the event. The difference between PTS and PTSD is that the symptoms get worse, last for months or even years and interfere with your day-to-day ability to function. People prefer to use the term disorder because it has more neutral connotations than the term mental illness.

- Complex-Post Traumatic Stress Disorder (C-PTSD) is a behavioral or mental pattern that exhibits features similar to both BPD and PTSD. People with C-PTSD have suffered prolonged, repeated trauma combined with a sense of being powerless to escape or end the trauma. Examples of people who receive a diagnosis of C-PTSD have experienced sexual, emotional or physical abuse; neglect in childhood; intimate partner violence; and kidnapping or hostage situations - or were indentured servants; placed into slavery; sweatshop workers; prisoners of war; concentration camp survivors; and defectors of cults or cult-like organizations.[11]

Let's unpack it a little further together.

--------

11 https://en.wikipedia.org/wiki/Complex_post-traumatic_stress_disorder

The BPD/PTSD Overlap

As the definitions show, there is often an overlap between BPD and PTSD and many people receive a dual diagnosis of both PTSD and BPD because both have their origins in traumatic events. Traumatic childhood events like abuse often manifest in the thoughts, feelings, and behaviors seen in BPD; these traumas place someone at a higher risk of developing PTSD later in life.

[Author side note: In my work as a PTSD recovery coach and through my relationships with many veterans, I find that many who enter the elite branches of the military do so because they have suffered childhood abuse. They don't ever want to be placed in a position of vulnerability again. Because of the stigma of sexual abuse, many never admit to having experienced it and never report it later on in life. The early trauma makes it nearly impossible for them to manage their military service PTSD effectively. The true-to-life movie *Antwone Fisher* deals with this subject.]

BORDERLINE PERSONALITY DISORDER (BPD)

This condition is often poorly explained. However, Dr. Frank Ochberg[12] does it very well:

"Borderline was intended, almost half a century ago, to be the boundary between psychosis and neurosis. Some people were observed to have difficulty managing anxiety (neurosis), but they also lost touch with reality (psychosis) when extremely distressed.

---

12 http://www.giftfromwithin.org/html/FAQ-Link-Between-PTSD-BPD-Bi-Polar.html

http://www.giftfromwithin.org/html/FAQ-Definition-of-PTSD.html

Unlike persons who have schizophrenia or bipolar disorder, they were usually free of prolonged episodes of disordered thinking or mood fluctuations. But they often had relatives diagnosed with these disorders (schizophrenia; bipolar). The very first criterion for giving the diagnosis is "frantic efforts to avoid real or imagined abandonment." Therapists who follow Freudian and similar theories look for significant events in the early stages of life, formative events, and they place great weight on such life-shaping experiences."

## POST TRAUMATIC STRESS DISORDER (PTSD)

The basic concept is this: You were a completely normal person, and then something dreadful happened. You didn't recover in several weeks; in fact, you now have a recognizable pattern of difficulty that lasted at least a month.

To have PTSD is to have a trauma memory that haunts you, that comes when you don't want it, that isn't always there but is there too often. And it is different from a *normal* memory of a terrible thing. Many of us have lived through natural disasters, the unnatural death of loved ones, abuse, humiliation, bullying and sudden, catastrophic loss. We were traumatized and maybe even victimized. We remember, and we hurt. But we are NOT plagued by any of the symptoms. We have autobiographical memory. The past feels as though it is in the past. We know the bad details. The bad details do not spring out at us every month, causing palpitations, nightmares, flashbacks, terror, or a sick thud in the chest. Without this category of unwanted re-experiencing, we do not have PTSD.

PTSD symptoms include:

- Recurrent and intrusive distressing recollections of the event, which may manifest in dreams of the event;

- Acting or feeling as if the traumatic event is recurring (includes a sense of reliving the experience, illusions, hallucinations, and dissociative flashback episodes, including those that occur upon awakening or when intoxicated); and

- Intense psychological distress when exposed to internal or external cues that symbolize or resemble an aspect of the traumatic event. This distress can also include physiological responses to internal or external cues, which is colloquially known as the *Fight or Flight Response.*

## COMPLEX - PTSD

Here is my take on all this: because of the stigma associated with BPD and because of the overlap between BPD and PTSD in the area of trauma, experts developed a new category of trauma-based PTSD called Complex-Post Traumatic Stress Disorder. This combination is the best of both worlds, as it were. In recent years, some suggest that BPD should be replaced with C-PTSD. The one thing that I feel is very distinct with C-PTSD is that it takes into account the tendency for re-victimization. Because of childhood abuse, someone with C-PTSD can be caught up in the cycle of ongoing abusive relationships, without the ability to recognize them or the internal capacity to break free from them.

# BROKEN IN HARD PLACES

She came she said

           Look at this

She came she said

           touch me here

She came she said

           kiss me here

She came she said

           put it here

She came she said

           don't tell anyone

She came she said

           they won't understand

She came she said

           again
           again
           again

She came

he said

           no
           mum
           it's wrong

Taken from *No Working Title: a Life in Progress* by Dr. John A. King, available at www.drjohnaking.com.

She came
He left
but it follows him
everywhere

shadow
on his soul

broken
in hard places

broken
in places not seen

## THE VICTIM NARRATIVE

I am not my past.
I am my future.

—Dr. John A. King

**Narrative:** An account of events, experiences; whether true or fictitious, the story or account.

**Victim:** A person who suffers from a destructive or injurious action or injury.

**Choice:** The act of choosing; the power, the right, the option to choose; something that is preferred.

*Are you your past or your future?*

At some point, we all have to ask ourselves, "Do I always want to be defined by myself or others as a victim?" You can go after the story of an over-comer, or you can have the story of a victim. Neither of those is dependent upon your experience in the past; they are dependent upon your view of yourself in the future.

The Victim Narrative develops when a person, in the telling or retelling of their story, continuously writes themselves in as the one who was wronged or harmed. People choose, for a broad range of reasons, to engage in a victim narrative. Maybe it's because they enjoy the attention they get, or maybe it's to get a better insurance payout on a car accident.

On the other hand, there are those who have been sexually abused, blown up by an IED, or gone bankrupt through no fault of their own, and never see themselves as a victim. Why the difference?

<u>Not My Past</u>

Humans like labels. When we assign labels, it means we can pigeon hole someone. It gives us parameters upon which we can blame or explain behavior without ever trying to understand it. "Don't worry about him, he was abused, he just gets that way sometimes."

When you allow someone to label you as a victim of sexual abuse or human trafficking, then everyone can expect you to be one or all of the following:

1. Suffering from BPD/PTSD
2. Depressed
3. Have an eating disorder - either too fat or too skinny
4. Probably be over-sexed or under-sexed

There can be what some see as rewards if they embrace this mindset. People look at you with gooey eyes and say, "Oh, that's so sad. I'm so sorry for you," and they mean it, and it feels awesome. Why? Because you probably never had any positive affirmation in your life. For example, perfect strangers want to have sex with you to "show you what real love is." True story.

The trade off is that buying into this way of thinking encourages a sense of fatalism. It takes your future out of your hands and puts it into the hands of the collective. I am not prepared to do that, and I don't think anyone else should be either.

*The past is a foreign country; they do things differently there.*

—LP. Hartley

We have within us the ability to re-create, re-cast, or re-feel events in our lives. Whenever we recall or retell an event, we can choose to view ourselves, the events, and even the outcomes in different ways. We can add a particular flavor or emphasis to these experiences. We tend to think of memories as movies when in reality they are more like painting. Think of it this way, when a moment is captured as a movie, the unedited form provides a perfect, storable, retrievable, shareable, accurate account of events and occurrences. The human memory is not like that. The human memory is more like a picture painted and repainted over and over again with every telling and retelling.

In your mind, you are attempting to retell or recount an event with accuracy, but depending on the audience or the desired outcome you will place a different emphasis on the tale. It might be a total redrawing of the memory, or it may just be the adding of a single different stroke. You may consciously or unconsciously (I talk about this in *The Magical Number Seven, Plus or Minus Two section*) color it in a certain way. The result however is that you have just changed that memory forever.

This phenomenon is why two people who witness the same event can recall it in two different ways. You cannot fact check your own memory. You can't store it externally on a hard drive, or in digital form to recall later. Every time you remember it, you *repaint* it. That is why eye-witness accounts are never identical. That is why it is good to physically record things —write them down at the time of the occurrence. Over time and under different circumstances, the way you recall them will change. Over time, if

you don't record them, if you don't capture them externally, then little by little the memories will become laced with embellishments. The narrative may change, details deleted, or emphases placed. These changes will take on a consistent flavoring, depending on the emotional, psychological, or even physiological state of the person recalling the events.

In light of this, let's look at The Victim Narrative.

If personality predisposes an individual, or if they will benefit in some way by casting themselves in the light or manner of a victim, then their recall of events will be filtered through that lens. A person with such predisposition, who has suffered greatly at the hands of another or as the result of some life event, will naturally re-cast any memory with them as the victim. The filtering may be subconscious, or it could be deliberate if there were some personal gain to be made, but the filtering will occur. This conscious or unconscious (refer to *The Magical Number Seven, Plus or Minus Two section*) choice is the filter that I call The Victim Narrative.

Even the statement "suffered greatly" is subjective. People have different pain tolerances, be it physical or emotional pain. Even a small amount of pain over a long enough period can become too much for someone to cope with - similar to the classic Chinese water torture.

Maybe another helpful way to say it is that "your perception is your reality." Perception does not make the reality. Perception allows one to craft the reality of their story. Perception is how you understand something. If your perception is that you are a victim, then you will be a victim. You not only will be a victim concerning this one tragedy or trauma, but also across the board

- it's a mindset. You will never find a parking space; the checkout attendants will always be rude; and you will never get a break, chance, or have any luck. All those things happen to other people, but not you because you are a victim. Being a victim will be the story of your life; it is how you see everything and what you expect in every situation.

## YOUR PAST WILL EITHER CONFINE/DEFINE YOU OR REFINE YOU.

So herein lay my decision: "Would I be a man who is a victim of sexual abuse, OR would I be a boy, who had suffered abuse at the hands of women and men, who had grown into a man?

My conclusion was that my past would refine me; I would not allow it to confine or define me.

I wouldn't *run from* what happened to me; I would *run at* what had happened to me. I wouldn't be embarrassed by the scars my past caused; I would re-cast them as medals of Honor in my mind. I would wear them proudly, and I would talk about them openly.

And this all came very easily to me, and I never struggled one bit. <ROFL>

*What will be your next chapter?*

I look back on my early poetry writings, and they were harsh, hard, and angry. I have felt at times tempted to destroy them or disregard them, or not show them, but to do so would be dishonest. To do so would not allow others to benefit from the

process, the journey from brokenness to wholeness. To do so would be rewriting my past. When someone writes a poem, paints a picture or crafts a sculpture, they are, for all time giving voice to that particular event. I didn't want to paint over historical fact; I wanted to embrace it.

Here lies the challenge and the beauty of "Art as Therapy." By using art as part of your process, you can either embed The Victim Narrative further into your life or make your way out. Like small steppingstones, every piece of art will create a path that you can walk on. A path to see your life and yourself that hopefully can be followed by others to lead them out of their mess.

*What makes a triumph magnificent? Is it not the tragedy and obstacles overcome along the way?*

I read/hear some peoples' stories, or see their art, and in 20 years of telling, it hasn't changed. It is as dark and hopeless at the end as it was at first recall. Many people with PTSD struggle with this. They have allowed their art or story to embed The Victim Narrative into their lives instead of freeing them from it. They didn't build a path forward in their lives. Instead, they built a wall around themselves that has held them captive.

Someone once accused me of using my art to perpetuate my victimhood. When asked, the person had only seen two or three pieces of my work. When I showed them my current work, they refused to believe that I could be the author. Why? Because it is so very different, it is full of redemption, new hope and a new love. It is full of possibility and talk of a future - and that is how it should be.

Maybe my later work won't be recognized or counted with the same weight that my darker, earlier pieces were. But why does that matter? I never embraced art to enshrine my tragedy, but to make sense of it. I ran to art to give expression and faces to the demons that haunted me not to celebrate them; instead to vanquish them. YOU CANNOT DEFEAT AN ENEMY YOU DO NOT KNOW.

**Imagine this:** You are standing in front of a 6'x8' landscape painting of incredible beauty. One section of the scene is the depiction of an old, broken-down house. You are brought into the room blindfolded and placed with your nose about 2" from the portion of the picture that is the house. When you open your eyes, all that consumes your vision is the grisly, destructive scene of that house.

Over the next 15 minutes, you slowly walk backwards away from the picture until you can see and admire the beauty of the whole landscape. The broken house and all its horrors are still there; nothing has changed that. What has changed is your perspective. The house is now one small part of the overall picture.

When you suspect that your art or your words or your thought patterns have enshrined your past for you, instead of carrying you farther away from it towards wholeness and health, you must ask yourself the question, "Have I embraced The Victim Narrative, or am I writing my next chapter?"

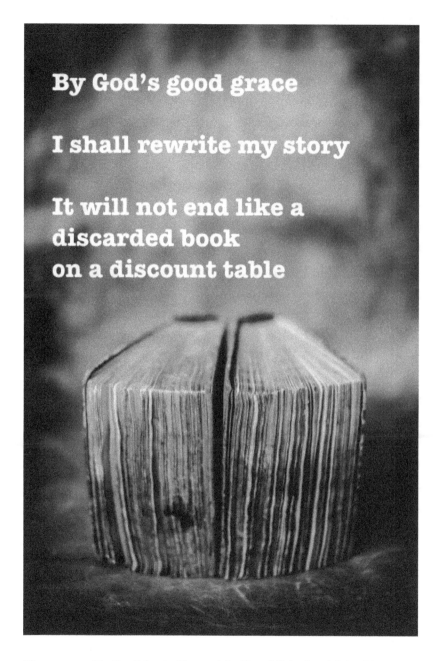

By God's good grace

I shall rewrite my story

It will not end like a
discarded book
on a discount table

Meme created by Dr. John A. King, originally published at drjohnaking.com.
Photo by Kiwihug on unsplash.com

## MEL'S TURN

From the outside looking in, the days with Mona seemed to be some of the hardest that John had. He was slogging it out. Fighting his past, his thoughts, his fears, and paranoia — taking on all the demons at once in an epic battle. And battles are messy. Battles rage on without a thought for their surroundings, and non-participants must take cover or become casualties.

What John needed in this war for his future were allies. He found one in Mona — she was a munitions specialist, handing him weapon after weapon for the fight. I saw the battle begin, and I knew I didn't want to take cover. I wanted to help. I cared about him, believed in him and saw too many of his so-called friends running for the hills. I didn't want to become a casualty, but my challenge was getting John to see that I was an ally. Understandably, he didn't trust easily.

So I just hung in there. Showed up every day, whether there was anything for me to do or not (we worked together). I had a friend say to me once, "Mel, you earned, through patience and hard work and loyalty, your place in John's life." That sounds nice, and I appreciate the sentiment so much, but the day-to-day was a little messier than that. I came to the fight with my own set of demons, inadequacies and imperfections. So there we were. Soldiers in the middle of a fight aren't always polite to one another, and they don't take the time to explain things. We developed a bit of emotional shorthand that might confound onlookers. But I didn't care. We saw progress.

Trust continues to be an issue for John. I see him decide to trust me over and over on small things and big things. It's always a

decision that he has to deliberately make. Literally, down to the night before we got married, he said he didn't want to do it. He said he thought he loved me, and he knew he was the one who proposed. And yes, he'd written me all this wonderfully romantic poetry, told me to cancel the lease on my apartment, made a guest list and ordered a food truck; but he didn't know if he wanted to be married again. He wasn't sure he could trust me — to love him, to care for him, to stay around. I was like, "Well, my love, we'll have one heck of a nice party tomorrow anyway ... you can decide right before I put on my dress, okay?"

Obviously, John has plenty of reasons not to trust anyone. It's best not to take things like that personally, but I don't always get it right. The natural (human, NOT helpful!) response is something like, "WTF! I'm perfectly trustworthy!"

And sometimes that's the response he gets. More often than not, though, if I stay calm, if I am patient, it gives him time to make the decision to trust.

It's important to mention that I have never seen John as having any disability or mental disorder. That causes me to expect him to cope. Sometimes I have to deal with my surprise when he doesn't, but on the whole, I think my bumbling approach has been helpful. I know sometimes he sees me as stupidly optimistic, but this stupid optimism allows him to fail and recover and doesn't expect him to fail the same way next time.

John is tough on himself *all the time*. He never allows himself to go down the victim path, and he doesn't tolerate it in others. This approach makes him an excellent coach and keeps my pity-parties confined to the length of a hot bath or a cup of coffee!

## CHAPTER THREE

# Kangaroos in the Top Paddock

A question that sometimes drives me hazy: am I or are the others crazy?

—Albert Einstein

Sane is boring.

—R.A. Salvatore

It seems to me that really crazy people don't think they're crazy. Why would you?

—Elizabeth Chandler

So I had all this head knowledge but still no knowledge about my head.

I had done lots of reading about physical changes that happened to the brain with a head injury from football or the battlefield. I was aware of the developing science around the impact of emotional trauma and how the brain functioned and processed things post-trauma. But I wasn't reading anything on childhood sexual abuse and its impact on brain function. There was talk about PTSD and its impact on brain anatomy, but no one knew if it were permanent. No one was taking this science over to the area of childhood sexual abuse.

In 2016, I travelled to Atlanta for a business meeting to connect with some people working with innovative medical technology. Just after lunch, we were sitting, joking around, and someone suggested: "Why don't you scan the Australian to see if he has kangaroos hopping around up there?"

We all had a great laugh, and I agreed. What my business associate was referencing was a new technology they were using on veterans who were diagnosed with severe cases of PTSD. This technology scanned the brain and produced a graphical interpretation of brain function and brain health. The system was designed to measure and help manage cognitive function and impairment *objectively*. It did this by detecting subtle variations in brain activity and performance. It was proving to be a great aid to veterans in helping them understand their PTSD. What the technology couldn't do however was tell if the PTSD caused the changes to the brain's function, or if an injury caused it on the battlefield. They never scanned anyone with PTSD who had not served in the military.

The doctor who was operating the system took what looked like a shower cap or a colander that had a bunch of probes hanging off it. He attached the probes to my scalp and the scanner to his laptop. I sat there looking like something from *Young Frankenstein*. The guys thought it was awesome. They couldn't wait to "see the roos hoping around." The jokes were bad, crude and very funny. The doc pushed the GO button, and I stepped through the assessment while everyone else went back to the business at hand.

Bro - You Got Issues

The test timed out, and the doctor was halfway through a comment to everyone else in the room when the results came on the screen. His face went blank and he was dead quiet. Everyone looked at him and he just looked at the screen. He typed something, looked at it again, and then very solemnly said in his best 'there is nothing to worry about' voice, "How about we step outside and have a talk?"

Out in the foyer, he wanted to know about my extensive military background. It took me a while to convince him that I didn't have one. He then wanted to know how many years I had been playing professional football. I told him I hadn't seen a game let alone played in one. He refused to believe me. He went on to explain that what he was seeing was one of the worst cases of PTSD-related brain inactivity/activity he had ever seen. He said that my entire frontal lobe was completely blue and that other parts that should be blue were completely red. [See Figure 1]

"Doc, what does blue mean?" I asked, "Is that good or bad?"

With glorious clinical detachment, he said, "Simply put, it's not working, your brain's not working. The front third of your brain,

your frontal lobe, is so incredibly deficient, that there are other parts just working overtime to compensate. We have only seen this in veterans with the most severe trauma following extended periods in theaters of war. This result is unheard of for someone who is not a veteran. What happened to you?"

*Figure 1:* My Brain Scan Results

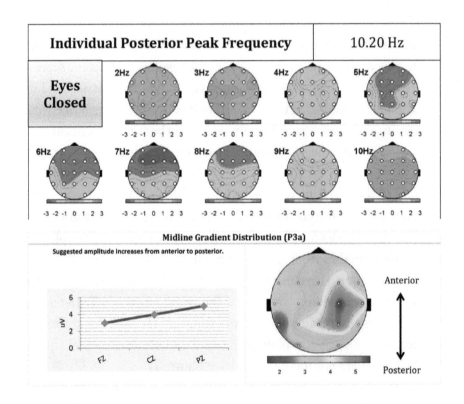

So we took a seat and over the next hour and a Bourbon (or two), I told him my story. Apparently, for the doctor and his company, I was the first person they tested with C-PTSD as a result of sexual abuse; and it was the first time they recorded a brain scan of a severe case of PTSD unrelated to either professional sports or battlefield injury. It opened up a whole new world of business opportunity for him and his company. For me, it brought incredible relief. I could see on the screen that my brain functioned differently than others.

I had been told time and time again I should just "Get over my shit and stop acting like a child." One of my personal favorites, "You're just making all this up, you're a liar, you're just doing this to get attention." I had been told that it was all in my head - and now I had proof that it was.

The years of abuse and trauma had lead to a physical change in my brain's ability to cope with and process everything from emotion to memories. The panic attacks, the paranoia, and the anxiety were not just the raving of a "crazy, self-indulgent retard." They were the physical manifestation of a physical, neurological condition. It gave me evidence that I wasn't crazy in a bad sense. I was crazy in a good, "I told you so, now fuck off" sort of way and something I could grab onto. I was sick and tired of all the tree-hugging, namby-pamby, crystal belly button navel-gazing bullshit that everyone insisted was the answer to the issue of dealing with my past or my illness.

The following weeks of study and learning consisted of five parts hope and five parts despair, which gave me a better idea of what the impact of the abuse had been. My concern was: *how do you correct a brain function issue?* I know my brain had self-

compensated, but how do I fix the broken bits? How do I relearn the skill sets I need? How do I build forward? How do I prevent it from worsening? PTSD now had a real physiological, not just psychological, face to it. I wasn't just dealing with some *feelings;* I was dealing with brain damage. I was dealing with changes on a biological level that affected a full range of emotional and physical responses and behaviors.

These brain scans and the test results also freed me from a lot of guilt, which brought a lot of peace. I now knew why I did some of the things I did and reacted the way I reacted. As the mighty Star-Lord said, "I might be a dick, but I wasn't 100% A-hole." I wasn't trying to justify bad or immoral behavior, but now I knew why I went from one extreme to another. I understood why I reacted and responded the way I did, especially in the early days of John-A-Geddon, and why some things that used to be incredibly easy were now incredibly hard. I now had a new enemy. Once again, I had an identifiable opponent that I could climb into the ring with, one that I could train to beat. It was GAME ON.

## FRONTAL LOBE, FRONTAL LOBE, WHEREFORE ART THOU

Whether you believe you can, or whether you believe you can't, you're right.

—Henry Ford

The majority of reading and talking with people I had done was around the area of PTSD and its impact on veterans, so I was able to relate, in theory, to the results of my brain scans. But I didn't have a reliable enough connection to be comfortable appropriating that research to my own experience. Once the brain scans confirmed an identical biologically similarity between my brain function/dysfunction in the area of PTSD to that of a veteran, I was able to take over 200 years of research and thought and apply it to my situation. I concentrated my immediate efforts on trying to understand what these brain scans meant. I wanted to know not only how they could help me figure out why I found something difficult or why I responded in a certain way, but also why I seemed almost *gifted* in other areas.

The brain scan showed that I had a massive decrease in activity or functionality in my frontal and temporal lobe. It also revealed that the right side of my brain, the seat of creative cognition, was running overtime to compensate for what the left side wasn't doing. What follows is a summary of what I learned and how it helped me.

## The Temporal Lobe

The temporal lobe is responsible for processing the input from both your eyes and ears. It is responsible for long-term memory along with being responsible for receiving and interpreting sound, sight and smell - the sensory memories. You may have heard of the term *trigger*. For someone with PTSD, a *trigger* happens when a person encounters a sight, sound, and/or smell that reminds them of an event.

An essential part of the temporal lobe is the amygdala. The amygdala evaluates a stressful situation and decides for the brain what action should take place for self-preservation. It's the part that sends out the danger signals. If you've heard of the term *Fight or Flight Response,* the amygdala is responsible for those responses.

Areas of the temporal lobe are also responsible for a person's ability to navigate spatially and to remember a place they have been before. People with damage in this area are often unable to process where they have been and where they are going, and they are often easily disoriented.

Another key part of the temporal lobe is the hippocampus. The hippocampus is essential for memory formation, storage, and retrieval. It handles learning and memory function; it's also designed to calm the *Fight or Flight Response* in the amygdala. Because it is reduced in size due to the impact of trauma, the hippocampus in someone with PTSD is unable to calm the amygdala down when there is a perceived danger. In other words, the hippocampus can't counterbalance the *Fight or Flight Response.* Instead of regulating memories, it involuntarily retrieves memories

when triggered by a stimulus and has a central role in someone re-living or re-experiencing those events as a flashback or as a nightmare. Another side effect for me due to the left temporal lobe not functioning as it should have is: I developed an issue with remembering and comprehending what was said to me. Simply put, I couldn't understand shit sometimes. People would stand right in front of me talking, and all I would want to know is, "Where is my Babel Fish when I need it?"

## The Frontal Lobe and the Prefrontal Cortex

The frontal lobe is responsible for things like:

- Problem-solving and decision making
- Controlling emotions and behavior
- Planning, organizing, memory, and attention

The frontal lobe helps regulate appropriate social responses and social behavior. In those with PTSD, the frontal lobe is less active. When this happens, people tend to become withdrawn. They avoid crowds, individuals or places that might cause a *triggering* event. When the frontal lobe is not working correctly, the possibility of high-risk behaviors like hyper-sexuality, drugs and alcohol-related issues are just about a certainty. Other higher risks are developing eating disorders, self-harm, and suicide.

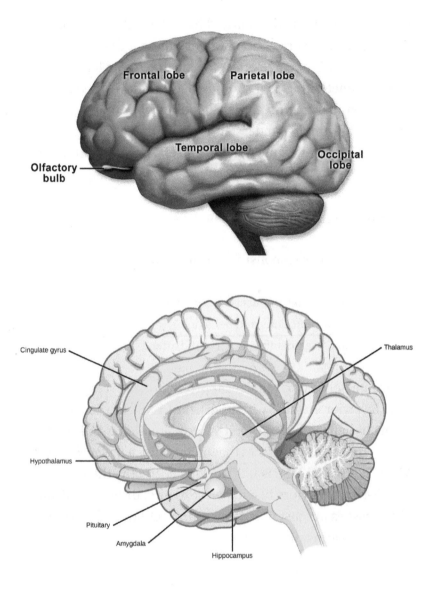

*Figure 2*: The Brain Lobes[13] [14]

13 https://commons.wikimedia.org/wiki/File:Blausen_0111_BrainLobes.png

14 https://commons.wikimedia.org/wiki/File:Figure_35_03_06.jpg

It's All One System

The brain, like every other living thing, is a system made up of many parts [see *Figure 2*]. These elements are all tied together and are designed to operate in unison and concert with each other. When they are not running as they were intended to, the whole system will either underreact or overreact in an attempt to compensate. For example, when you are experiencing a flashback, and the frontal lobe (which regulates behavior) is unable to override the hippocampus (memory function and recall), it cannot signal the amygdala (the part that gets massively agitated) that the danger you feel is imaginary or just a memory. What happens is that your senses heighten and you are unable to stop jumping to conclusions and assuming the worst. You end up being either fearful and cowering, or rageful and angry. The system is not operating according to the designer's manual.

Here are four scenarios that might give you a picture of how this has played out in my life. It might give you insight for your own situation, or examples of what it could look like for you or someone you love.

**Scenario #1:** *Fight or Flight Response in an emotionally charged environment*

You forget something about your children's activities or schedule. The conversation you have with your spouse over this issue is becoming laced with emotion, and you're starting to get confused with specifics. You're verbally assaulted and insulted. The more your partner pushes you, the mental processing you need for speech starts to shut down, and you start to stutter badly. You're now told to stop faking the stuttering and that you only do that

for attention. Your ability to hear and comprehend closes down further. You end up on the floor in a vulnerable position because the only alternative is to lash out. There is no in-between.

Someone is now standing over you screaming that you're a retard, you're useless, you'll never amount to anything, you're not really a man. You are instantly transported back to a childhood scenario where the same words and tone were used. You are 11 years old and surrounded by people who are about to violate you.

There comes a point that when a person is unable to *flight*, they will *fight*. Their response at being pushed too far is pure survival instinct.

For someone without PTSD, it might look like this: You have a memory of an unfortunate childhood event, let's call that bucket #1. One day you get into an argument with your spouse, let's call that bucket #2. If you don't have PTSD, you can have an argument in the now, bucket #2, and memories of bucket #1 never enter your mind. You can even be having an argument and be thinking how this sounds like something you once went through, but both buckets still stay separate.

If you have PTSD, then you start in bucket #2 and you are not thinking about anything else. You are totally in that moment on a conscious level. However, on an unconscious level (refer to *The Magical Number Seven, Plus or Minus Two section*), bucket #1 is starting to vibrate. It's like ripples start to appear on what was a very calm and undisturbed bucket of memories. If the situation de-escalates, then the ripples subside.

If the argument in bucket #2 continues and something happens or is said that triggers the memories in bucket #1, then an uncontrollable eruption takes place. Bucket #1 knocks over bucket #2 and all the emotions mingle together and flood your mind. The two situations become completely indistinguishable for the PTSD sufferer, and the *fight* response takes over from the *flight* response.

The resulting response can be borderline feral as the person is once again caught up re-living past experiences in the present moment.

**Scenario #2:** *Unexpected Triggers*

I remember sitting with Melissa one evening. We had a great day, a beautiful afternoon and were watching an old Steve McQueen movie. I told her I had never seen it, but had always wanted to. About 45 minutes into the movie, I started getting agitated. Ten minutes later I got up and was stomping around the house checking the doors and the windows. I began screaming about how we had to be safe, and the doors should never be left unlocked and, "WHY THE FUCK ARE THESE WINDOWS OPEN?!?" I was out of control. I mean totally out of control. I was raging hysterically, screaming, fearful that we were vulnerable and someone could be coming to get us at any moment to hurt us.

I had no memory of ever seeing that movie before, but part of my temporal lobe did. About an hour later the storm had started to subside, and while Melissa held me, I was able to tell her about the memories that the movie had triggered. I had been sexually violated while that movie played in the background. Up to that point, I never remembered that I had watched this film before. I never recollected seeing it. But the amygdala did. It associated

the movie, and apparently a particular set of scenes, with danger and fear. I went from calm and relaxed to the desperate need to protect myself and those I loved. This episode was nine years after the initial recall happened in 2008, and 41 years after I "saw" the movie for the first time.

**Scenario #3:** *Suicide - not a cry for help but an attempt to stop the pain*

I know I mentioned the issue of contemplating suicide earlier, in the Re-defining Normal section. I write about it again now because after I came to understand the nature of PTSD, I understood why I contemplated ending my life. As I repeat it here, I hope you can also see it in a different light.

I remember this period with great difficulty. To think that if I had taken my life, I would never have gotten to experience the life of love and possibility that I now wake to every day is absolutely tragic. I would have been a statistic and not a story.

Here are several things to consider before we have a look at this again:

- Men die by suicide 3.5 times more often than women – in 2016, 4 men committed suicide for every 1 woman.[15]
- In 2015, the highest rate of suicide was among white men (15.1%).[16]

---

- As many as 20% of veterans have PTSD. There are 18.8 million veterans.[17]
- A 2016 report by Veterans Affairs states that 20 veterans a day commit suicide.[18]
- The average life span of a person with BPD is 41 years. This is due to issues of addiction, risky behavior, suicide, or stress-related medical problems.[19]

I went through a time of evaluating suicide as an option. It was very calculating and cold. I was logically looking at it as an option. Depression or anxiety didn't drive me. I thought I'd be doing everyone a favor. My motive for contemplating suicide was because I was tired and ashamed at how I was hurting those who I was desperately trying to love. I just wanted the pain that I was causing to stop. This is overwhelmingly the case with PTSD sufferers, be they sexual abuse survivors or veterans.

After the tragedy of suicide, family members and friends will often say, "I never knew; they never said anything." And they wouldn't have, because many of the men and women I've spoken to who have contemplated suicide are the strongest I've ever known — mentally and physically. As a spouse or friend of someone with PTSD, I encourage you: ask the question, have a conversation, throw a lifeline. They may never use it, but "just in case" is always a good option to make available to them.

---

17 https://www.rand.org/news/press/2008/04/17.html

18 https://www.militarytimes.com/veterans/2016/07/07/new-va-study-finds-20-veterans-commit-suicide-each-day/

19 https://www.researchgate.net/publication/229080483_Life_expectancy_at_birth_and_all-cause_mortality_among_people_with_personality_disorder

# SUICIDE

Like a wet kiss
she asks for surrender

Like a soft whisper
she seduces

Like a lover
she promises to satisfy

Like a broken record
she sings the same song
the promise of peace

Rejected
like a cheap whore
she leaves disgusted

To return tomorrow to try again

Taken from *No Working Title: a Life in Progress* by Dr. John A. King, available at www.drjohnaking.com.

**Scenario #4:** *High-Risk behavior*

Engaging in high-risk behavior from the damage to my frontal lobe was not something I could ever have prepared for. I had been a Christian since I was 25, and I had always had a sense of right and wrong. When John-A-Geddon happened, all of that seemed to stop; I liken it to losing any sense of moral conscience or compass. High-risk behavior is defined as any "decision or behavior that carries with it the high potential for punishment or reward."[20] And nearly all of these behaviors have severe medical, legal, or interpersonal consequences.

For me, it didn't matter if it were alcohol, sex, violence, or extreme sport. Once it was riding my motorbike at 100 mph down a highway with the lights off at night, in the rain, dressed in shorts and a T-shirt. Another time it was flying a single engine plane into an ice storm to see if the emergency procedures I had learned applied - I know, mind-numbingly stupid-ass things. It didn't matter what it was, I needed and wanted to try it, because my internal regulator had stopped working. I knew on a cerebral level that I was going to hit a statistical or physical brick wall at some point, but that didn't stop me. Nothing inside me was telling me to stop or curb the behavior. I needed it. I needed the rush and the relief it gave me. It made me feel alive and in control. It filled my head with something other than the rubbish that seemed to flood it unabated; it gave me brief respite from the day-to-day struggle to survive.

---

20 Lawrence, Richard Jason, "PTSD and High-Risk Behaviors in Trauma Survivors" (2012). ETD Archive. Paper 408.

The day I realized I had to deal with my issue of risky behavior was the day I nearly got Mel killed.

I grew up on Sydney Harbor and water sport was just something we all did. It was no big deal, just life in a coastal city. I sailed throughout my youth and loved it. There is nothing like the freedom of a catamaran at high speed in heavy wind.

One day I decided to buy a catamaran and teach the kids and Mel how to sail on the lake by our house. Sounds very suburban and safe when I say it like that. What happened though was totally different.

I had been growing increasingly bored with myself and life. I was feeling the need for a rush and started looking for a boat. It didn't take me long to move from a suitable beginner/family tub to a racing catamaran. The catamaran I brought home one Sunday was a national champion, and it was rigged for speed and needed an experienced crew to sail it. I knew all of that and casually overlooked it.

The day I took Mel out, the wind was gusting to 25 knots, a tough sail for experienced hands. When it popped up on a single hull in the first five minutes as we tacked away from the dock, I yelled with delight. I had never sailed anything as fast or responsive in my life. I was so happy. This was it! This was the feeling, the rush, the risk and danger I had been missing.

[The thing with risky behavior-driven pursuits is that the probability of failure and its consequences are never factored in. I never really considered Melissa. This was all about me. Risky behavior doesn't come out of a selfish need or desire — the drive is something

far more primal and uncalculated. I've very intentionally done parachuting, para-flying, repelling, and spelunking - all very calculated. This drive was not like that.]

So the wind shifted and I miscalculated the position of my feet on the hull. That's right, 30 years since I last sailed, and I was out, fully stretched on a trapeze like an idiot. The catamaran nose-dived, Melissa was thrown off the boat, and I hit my head on the top of the mast as I was catapulted into the water.

In those conditions, it would have been tough even for an experienced crew of two or three to get it upright and going again. I struggled to right the boat by myself as I drifted farther and farther away from Melissa as she bobbed around in her life jacket.

Over the next 45 minutes, I would right the boat three more times, only to have it go over again. I was exhausted and concussed. I was eventually able to pick Mel up again and hand her over to the fire department in their boat (someone saw us from shore and called it in). They took her to shore while I sailed back in.

As I tacked my way back to shore, what I had just done hit me with full force. My behavior not only put myself at risk, it also put someone I loved and cared for very deeply at risk. I realized I wasn't just out of control, but that something inside me must be broken for me to act that way. I realized if I didn't fix whatever it was that had stopped working, I would never get well or be able to live productively, and someone I loved was probably going to get hurt.

Up until this point, I had been entirely focused on addressing external behaviors. I felt that if I stopped myself from behaving

in certain wrong ways, then I would naturally just start behaving in right ways. This was obviously not the case.

As I approached the shore, I came to the conclusion that the error laid not in my behavior, but my brain. The only real way to change an external action was to address the internal component that caused it. I needed to stop focusing on my behavior and start focusing on my thinking. My PTSD was brain-based, not body-based. I needed to think differently in order to start to live differently. Also, instead of being consumed with what I couldn't do, I needed to start focusing on what I could do.

This epiphany, I believe, started me up the other side of the dark valley that I found myself living in for seven years or so, and was the greatest gift I received from that day of sailing. That, and I knew I was going to sell that stupid boat as soon as my head stopped hurting.

## MEL'S TURN

We were about a month out from our wedding day when John had the brain scan. He sat me down (very seriously and ominously) and explained how his brain was broken. I'm pretty sure that's the word he used. He went on to say that I probably deserved someone better and that he understood if I wanted to call the whole thing off. My reply was something like, "Fuck off. I love your beautiful brain, and you (and it) are stuck with me." And that was that.

I had been reading about the brain for years, exploring concepts like elasticity, or the ability of one section of the brain to pick up the slack when injury occurs in another. Off and on, I had prayed specifically for John's brain for as long as I had known him. It wasn't a surprise to me that he had physiological effects from his childhood. Some part of me expected it, based on what little I knew about brain science. What we had now was just more information.

We now knew why he responded the way he did in certain situations and that helped us with what to expect. We could make adjustments. We could try to head off the high-risk behavior, or recognize it and do our best to deal with whatever concern was behind it. (And modify our approach to doing sports together, for example: selling the sailboat!) I could also help John when he encountered an unexpected trigger. When he goes off the rails, it can come with what seems like a very personal verbal attack. With what we now knew about his brain, I could recognize that behavior as a fight response and do my best not to take it personally. I try to keep my body language very soft, move toward him (not away), speak softly, stay open, and do my best to help him see that he's

safe. We don't always do it perfectly, but our wins are outpacing our losses since we got the scan.

While I continue to pray for his brain to heal and pathways to re-grow, we continue to manage everything together. My goals every day for John are the following: rest (getting a good sleep), connection (spending some quality time together), and smiles (I do my utmost to get him to smile at least once a day). He is plenty driven enough to handle the work and household goals for both of us - I focus on keeping him healthy - and sailboat-free.

## CHAPTER FOUR

# Living From the Inside-Out

Contentment is a flower from heaven that needs to be cultivated.

—Charles Spurgeon

Human beings, by changing the inner attitude of their minds, can change the outer aspects of their lives.

—William James

It is never too late to become what you might have been.

—George Elliot

As I laid in bed for the next day or so with the worst concussion I ever had, I noticed this strange re-occurring thought playing

over and over again ... *"I hope Mel didn't tell anyone about the sailing,"* and, *"How am I going to explain to people that I'm selling the boat?"* I don't remember thinking, *"How is Mel?"* (I know — that's messed up.)

My normal reaction to that line of thought would have been, *"That's bullshit John, you got to stop thinking that way,"* but this time that wasn't it. What I started to ask myself was, "Why are you even thinking that way? What is driving you from the inside to have that outward thought?"

Between praying for my head to terminally explode or the headache to subside, I realized this obsession with external behavior inhibited any real and lasting progress when it came to dealing with my PTSD. I hadn't engaged in an exercise of personal growth and development, I engaged in a program of attempted behavioral modification. I was so concerned with living up to other people's expectations and standards, trying to be normal for them, that I wasn't spending any time on making the internal changes that would produce long-term results.

Even after everything I'd been through in my personal life, all that I lost and suffered, I realized I was still more concerned with what people thought of my poor sailing instead of nearly drowning my future wife. My conclusion was that I, like most others I knew, had been trained to live, love, experience life, and face challenges from the outside-in.

From observation, most of our lives seem to track like this: Growing up and in school, we are taught how to fit in, how to conform to social rules and society's standards. We are encouraged to make choices in life, but with those choices, make as few waves as possible.

We are taught that external behavior should be the regulator for internal values. We are told that how we portray ourselves on the outside is more important than who we are and what we believe on the inside. (Remember high school? A couple thousand kids all dressing and acting the same to prove to everybody they were unique individuals? Grownups do exactly the same.)

In our 20's, we are busy building a career based on the expectations that others often have for us. Unfortunately, some of those desires arose from someone else's lack of fulfillment. For example, Daddy wasn't the lawyer he wanted to be, he worked in construction; therefore you have to be the lawyer. Mom wanted to play in an Amish rock band, but there weren't any, so you were made to play the glockenspiel.

In our 30's most of us continue on this path of least resistance. We never stop to ask ourselves the questions: "Am I fulfilled? Am I on the right path? Do I even like this crappy job?" Instead of having a deep sense of value, fulfillment and strong, connected relationships, we end up with a family, a mortgage and a growing sense of frustration about a life and situation that we don't feel we can control.

Then, when most of us hit our 40's and 50's, we seem to stop and do one of two things:

1). Re-examine and refocus our lives.
2). Live our remaining days as victims and inflict our frustrations on others.

The challenge with being reared this way is that it forces us into a situation where we end up being unauthentic people,

living unauthentic lives in shallow, unauthentic one-dimensional relationships. Our whole focus is on external behaviors and acceptance instead of internal growth and development, or that's how I felt.

As I laid there, I was faced with two questions:

1). How do I get that stupid dog next door to stop barking long enough so my headache can subside?
2). Where do I start?

My epiphany (aka near death experience) on the boat was that in order to live differently I had to think differently. I had been a student of the Bible for years, so I knew a bad heart produced bad things and a good heart produced good things; and I had seen Paycheck (Ben before he was the Bat), so I understood the basic principals of reverse engineering.

So that's just what I did. I started with the simple question: "How do I change the way I think so I can change the way I live?"

## THE MAGICAL NUMBER SEVEN – PLUS OR MINUS TWO

The moment you doubt you can fly, you cease forever to be able to do it.

—Peter Pan

In 1956, George Miller released a paper titled, *The Magical Number Seven—Plus or Minus Two*. Miller discovered that, depending on a person's mood or mindset, their conscious mind could hold seven plus or minus two bits of information at one time. For example, if someone was feeling good or optimistic, they could hold a total of nine things in their mind. If they were feeling negative, or they were not interested in something, they could only retain five things in their mind. In his study, he found that the more a person focused on something they didn't like, the less they were able to think about anything else except for those things they didn't like or that bothered them.

My conclusion was that if you concentrate enough on negative thoughts, you become oblivious to any other possibilities. In my case, the years of focusing on negative behavior I needed/wanted to change was having the exact opposite effect on what I wanted. When I combine Miller's study with what I discovered was the role of the unconscious mind, I came to the conclusion that YOU BECOME WHAT YOU THINK ABOUT.

## The Role of the Unconscious (subconscious) Mind

Although it is often used, the subconscious is not a proper psychological term, according to Harvard Health Publications.[21]

There are three types of consciousness:

1). Conscious
2). Preconscious
3). Unconscious (This is what most people are referring to when they say subconscious).

The conscious is what you perceive, your controlled thought.

The preconscious is what you can easily focus on and bring up quickly from memory.

The unconscious is what is going on "underneath the surface," without us being consciously aware.

*Good Air In, Bad Air Out*

Have you ever noticed that you don't have to think about breathing? Your body's simple request for more oxygen generates an automatic response. It is an unconscious activity, or rather, an activity you're not consciously aware of. Not only does the unconscious mind control the running of our bodies, but it can also have a tremendous impact on the results we get in every aspect of our

---

21 https://www.health.harvard.edu/blog/unconscious-or-subconscious-20100801255

conscious life. To achieve any success, we must endeavor to align both our conscious and our unconscious minds with our goals.

The conscious and unconscious minds excel at different things. The conscious mind is like the top 10% of an iceberg; the unconscious is the other 90%. One of the roles of the unconscious mind is to preserve and manage memories. It holds some, suppresses some, and keeps some memories always circling through your conscious mind.

Ready and Burton, in their book *Neuro-linguistic Programming for Dummies*, suggest that the unconscious mind cannot process negatives. It can only treat everything as a positive or active emotion. It works like this: if you say to yourself, "I don't want to be bitter or angry," it doesn't register the "don't." The unconscious mind interprets this statement or thought as "I want to be bitter and angry." It does not hear the negative declaration, only the positive action.

If you say, "I don't want to be poor," it hears, "I want to be poor." If you say, "I don't want to be sick," it hears, "I want to be sick." I know, total head trip.

I found this distressing at first, but quickly realized I could turn this quirk into a powerful ally by reprogramming how I thought about myself, how I talked about myself, and how I talked to others. I realized I couldn't program my mind with feelings; it just won't work. I couldn't try and *feel* good about myself or my future. Instead, I had to work with that weird little quirk of my unconscious and start to develop positive statements about myself, my life, and my future.

For example, instead of talking about what I felt I didn't have, I started to talk about what I knew I wanted and the sort of person I wanted to be:

- I am happy.
- I am a peaceful person.
- I am prosperous.
- I am healthy.
- I am a good husband.
- I am a good friend.
- I am a good parent.

I now understood that my unconscious mind was a lean, mean, learning machine; but it needed direction. The beautiful thing was it wanted to learn, and it was programmable. I realized my unconscious mind could be the greatest aid to inner peace and motivation if I programmed it correctly. I came to believe that if I fed it with possibilities and the right input, I could completely reprogram it. As a result, I could change the nature of my behavior, or the fruit of my life.

## REBOOTING MY SYSTEM

Recognizing that my internal guidance system was broken and that I was battling both my conscious and unconscious minds, I realized I needed to focus my energies on activities and re-establishing some life parameters not based on feelings but rather on actions. In other words, I needed to "fake it till I make it." I needed to make everything a positive action, based on a positive thought, until the deliberate behavior moved from a conscious effort to the unconscious mind.

Now this will all sound very cold and calculating, and to a great extent, it was. I wasn't waiting to be moved by emotion or desire; I was deciding to change my life and plotting a course accordingly. I was going to focus on three areas: my heart, my arse, and my head.

Getting my arse into gear.

I had been a gym rat all my life. It didn't matter what sport I played or participated in, be it rugby, karate, or boxing, lifting up and putting down heavy things was always a part of my training. But just going to the gym wasn't enough. I needed something that would consume my mind and exhaust me physically. Something I would have to focus on every day of the week. I found that in bodybuilding.

Bodybuilding requires so much mental, emotional and physical effort that it gave me very little time for anything else. With all the effort I was putting in at the gym, I didn't want to end up injured, so I stopped doing stupid stuff - well, most of it. I couldn't stay up late or go out because I needed to sleep, and I was so bloody tired anyway. I had to curb my drinking and watch my diet because

I now had goals. I wanted to qualify for the Masters, Over 50's, and Nationals, which I did.

Bodybuilding was an essential part of my recovery process because it enabled me to reframe my world and behavior in a deliberate, positive way. I changed my responses from *"I can't, I don't feel up to it,"* to *"I won't, I have goals and a focus."* That small shift made a massive impact.

<u>Dealing with my head. First up, ATTITUDE.</u>

David G. Myers, professor of Psychology at Hope College, said in his book, *Pursuit of Happiness* (p. 48): "Without minimizing catastrophe, the consistent and astonishing result is that the worst emotional consequences of bad events are usually temporary."

Myers quotes the life of W. Mitchell as an example:

"In 1971, he was burned, nearly killed, and left fingerless from a freak motorcycle accident. Four years later tragedy struck again. This time he was paralyzed from the waist down in a small plane crash. Though disfigured, he chose not to buy the idea that happiness requires handsomeness. 'I am in charge of my spaceship. It is my up, my down. I could choose to see this situation as a setback or a starting point.'"

Mitchell is a successful investor today, an environmental activist, and a speaker who encourages people to step back from their misfortunes. Take a wider view and say, "Maybe that isn't such a big thing after all! Before I was paralyzed there were 10,000 things I could do; now there are 9,000. I can either dwell on the 1,000 I've lost or focus on the 9,000 I have left."

<u>Next up, THE ISSUE OF SELF-SABOTAGE.</u>

I would love to say my recovery process went perfect and that I didn't stumble, fall, or screw up along the way; but, I can't. In the last two years, I have:

- torn both biceps off the bone;
- ripped a pectoral muscle;

- broken one ankle;
- dislocated a hip;
- narrowly avoided breaking my neck in a major mountain biking incident; and
- was engaged in that sailing event that we now laugh about. (Sorry babe, still feeling rather poorly about that one.)

I now realize I was doing things to sabotage my progress. Sometimes I put myself there and sometimes I allowed myself to be led by someone else. Self-sabotage is one of the symptoms that people experience when their unconscious conflicts with their conscious mind.

*Super Villain*[22]

*How do we self-sabotage?* Well, we listen to our unconscious mind. I realized that a negative unconscious mind is like an

---

22 https://simple.wikipedia.org/wiki/Villain#/media/File:Villainc.svg

obnoxious Super Villain. The Super Villain of self-sabotage sees itself as a superhero who is trying to cocoon us from previous painful experiences. Your unconscious mind wants to bring back memories and snapshots of the past to preserve and protect us from angst and emotional pain that we've suffered. The unconscious mind reminds us of what happened the last time we tried and failed or stumbled, and how much it hurt. When you allow the negative emotion and the negative memory to dominate your mind, you are reliving your past, one bitter and hurtful memory at a time. The only way around this is to re-program your mind with a positive memory.

Growing up, Fred and Rosemary told me day after day that I was "Captain Concrete - thick and dense." I often heard, "How come you're not smart like your sister? You'll never amount to anything; you're too stupid." In my later years, when things were at their lowest, I was repeatedly told that I would die lonely and alone because I was sick and incapable of knowing or experiencing love.

All of these things hurt; and to be honest, they still do at times. When the feeling of not being smart enough or good enough to be cared for or loved, come back to me, I sit down and remind myself how it felt to graduate high school. I remember how it felt to receive my post-graduate degrees. And, I remind myself how it felt to hear Melissa say "Yes!" when I asked her to marry me (bloody scary, but that isn't the point.)

I found the greatest secret for eliminating the inferiority complex, which is another term for deep and profound self-doubt, was to overflow my mind with a strong belief in myself and a committed belief in my future. I am not talking about flights of fancy, but about focusing on passions, dreams, and a vision for your life and

future. I focused on the feeling, the emotion, and the memories that came with those degrees and that "Yes!" from Melissa. The knowledge that I am lovable, intelligent, and a decent person anchored me as a man. Every day it was a choice to either build up feelings of insecurity, or build up feelings of security based on what I thought about.

Set it alight and watch it burn.

When one burns one's bridges, what a very nice fire it makes.

—Dylan Thomas

Burning a bridge was a practice used by great Roman and Greek generals. When they landed on an enemy's beach or crossed a bridge into enemy territory, they would set fire to their boats or burn the bridges behind them. There was no way for them to retreat. No way for them to go back. No retreat. No surrender.

That's what I did. I threw things out. I cancelled memberships. I stopped returning calls and cut off relationships. I went so far as to quit a job, all because they were not a positive influence and were not going to help me get to where I needed to go.

Getting my heart back in the game.

If my internal moral compass was broken, I needed external guidelines. I needed an anchor for my soul - something to stop me from drifting morally. An anchor is only useful if it's attached to something external from the boat. I started to read and re-read my Bible with fresh eyes. What my Bible gave me was the context for my day-to-day life with parameters and guard-rails for my decision-making. In a given situation, it wasn't a matter

of me *feeling* like I should do the right thing because I didn't feel anything. I made decisions that were based on what was best for myself and those I loved.

King Solomon wrote, "As a man thinks in His heart, so is he."[23] The Hebrew word for *heart* can mean "living being" or "inner/ living being of a man," or even "that which breathes." However you want to interpret the translation, it sure is different than the English definition[24]: "A hollow muscular organ that pumps the blood through the circulatory system by rhythmic contraction and dilation."

Here comes the weird stuff, I mean "freaking-me-out, my-head-exploding weird stuff."

In spring 2002 the *Journal of Near-Death Studies* published a study titled, "Changes in Heart Transplant Recipients that Parallel the Personalities of Their Donors."[25] The study consisted of open-ended interviews with 10 heart or heart-lung transplant recipients, their families or friends, and the donor's families or friends.

What the researchers discovered was the heart has a system of neurons, or a neurological system similar to that of the brain. The way the heart processes information was very similar in some ways to the brain. In fact, the heart had something called

---

23 Proverbs 23:7 (KJV)

24 New American Oxford Dictionary, https://en.oxforddictionaries.com/ definition/heart

25 Pearsall, P., Schwartz, G.E.R. & Russek, L.G.S. Journal of Near-Death Studies (2002) 20: 191. https://doi.org/10.1023/A:1013009425905

a cellular memory. The conclusion of the study found that both the brain and the heart process and store memory. The brain processed information by taking in facts via the senses and filing those facts away as mental images. The heart did something similar. However, the heart's filing method wasn't based on fact, but based on feelings. The heart attached an emotion to every piece of information that it recorded. *The heart is an emotional memory of what happens in your life.*

Sounds farfetched, doesn't it? It gets weirder from here on out.

Dr. Paul Pearsall was one doctor involved in this research, and he collected accounts from 73 heart transplant patients and 67 organ transplant patients and published them in various books and medical journals.[26]  Here are some of his case studies:

1) Paul Oldam, a lawyer from Milwaukee, received the heart of a 14-year-old boy and inherited the young man's craving for Snickers, a candy he had never liked before.

2) A man of 25 received a woman's heart and, to his girlfriend's delight, developed a desire to go shopping.

3) A 47-year-old white male factory worker received the heart of a 17-year-old black male student who was killed by a hit-and-run driver. Before the transplant, the older gentleman loved rock and roll music, but after the transplant, he had an unexplained passion

---

26 Paul Persall. The Heart's code: tapping the wisdom and power of our heart energy. New York; Broadway Books, 1999.

Paul Persall "Organ transplants and cellular memories " Nexus Magazine April/ May 2005;12:3

for classical music. Pearsall couldn't understand this. Surely a young black man would be a Hip-Hop guy? Upon reading police reports, he discovered the young man died clutching his violin on the way to his weekly lesson.

4) Then there is a case reported in the UK's Daily Mail[27]:

Bill Sheridan had retired from the catering industry and would have told you that he had drawing skills of a nursery-aged child - he was a stick figure artist. That was until he received a heart transplant. Days after the transplant, as part of his therapy, Bill was encouraged to draw, and immediately started producing drawings of wildlife and landscapes. When they asked about the donor, they found out the heart came from a 24-year-old stockbroker named Keith Neville. Keith's mother Donna said her son had drawn since he was 18 months old and "preferred art supplies over any other toy."

5) Then there is the case of Claire Sylvia, who Kate Linton mentions in her paper, Knowing By Heart.[28] On May 29, 1988, a woman named Claire Sylvia received the heart of an 18-year-old male who died in a motorcycle accident. Soon after the operation, Sylvia noticed some distinct changes in her attitudes, habits, and tastes. She found herself acting in a more masculine manner, strutting down the street (which, being a dancer, was a bit awkward for

27 "The Art Transplant" The Daily Mail March 31,2006.

28 Linton, Kate, Montgomery College Student Journal of Science and Mathematics (2003) Volume 2, "Knowing By Heart: Cellular Memory in Heart Transplants." http://citeseerx.ist.psu.edu/viewdoc/download?doi=10.1.1.535.2414&rep=rep1&type=pdf

her to explain). She began craving foods such as green peppers and beer, things she had always disliked before.

Sylvia even began having recurring dreams about a mystery man named Tim L., who she had a feeling was her donor. As it turns out, he was. Upon meeting the "family of her heart," as she put it, Sylvia discovered her donor's name was, in fact, Tim L. and that all the changes she had been experiencing in her attitudes, tastes, and habits closely mirrored those of Tim's. People thought the cases were just coincidences; many medical professionals were skeptical. Then came one instance they could not deny.

6) There was an 8-year-old girl who lived in the northwest United States who received a heart transplant from a 10-year-old girl who was murdered. The little girl who received the successful heart transplant began to have dreams that a man was chasing her and believed this man murdered her donor. Over time, the dreams that started out vague became clearer and clearer. It got to the point where these were no longer dreams, but terrifying nightmares. Her parents were very concerned because she couldn't sleep at night. They took her to a psychologist, who, after several sessions, declared she "could not deny the reality of what the child was telling her."

There came a point when the little girl started to describe things like the setting of the house and its contents. She described everything - right down to the individual who was chasing her in the dreams/nightmares. She described the place, the time, the clothes and even the weapon used to kill her donor.

Her parents and psychologist got the police involved.

Dr. Pearsall relates the story: "The police sketch artist came in, and they had the little girl describe everything that she was going through and everything that she saw. They actually were able to get a sketch of a man, a house and the interior of the house. This led police to the killer, who happened to be a neighbor of the little girl, the heart donor, who had been killed. They found evidence in the house that convicted, by trial and jury, the man of this murder."[29]

Besides freaking me out, I asked myself how this applied to me. I realized that our hearts hold memories, remember emotion, and can't tell which memory is real and which memory isn't. That's why horror movies work and why the recall in PTSD is so real.

For instance, you're sitting there with popcorn in a movie theater. The scariest thing there is the amount of cholesterol in the artificial butter. Then some hand puppet comes to life, starts killing people, and you jump so high popcorn covers everyone around you. None of it was real (except your wife dropping her soda in your lap and everyone thinking you peed yourself), but your heart and your mind cannot tell the difference between a real scare and an artificial one.

When you allow thoughts of fear, stress, or anxiety to take root in your heart and you start to dwell on them, you narrow your unconscious mind's ability to calculate possibilities, and you allow those fears to become a substance. As you think in your head and feel in your heart, so you are. Everything starts as a

---

29 Paul Persall. The Heart's code: tapping the wisdom and power of our heart energy. New York; Broadway Books, 1999.

thought, becomes a desire, then moves to a vision of your life and is outworked in some form of self-fulfilling prophecy or action.

Now start to run this series of thoughts alongside the information I outlined earlier on the operations of the brain and the emotional side of PTSD (see chapter 3). It all ties together and this is why deregulation and triggering are so extreme. This is why you can't just deal with PTSD as a mental issue. The function of the brain's memory is not the only factor in play. If all you are doing is trying to replace your mind's memories and not work on your heart's memories and harness them simultaneously, you will only see limited success.

When I first read this, I was overwhelmed with the thought that my workload just doubled. I now had to deal with my head AND my heart, but that wasn't what happened. When I put the link between head and heart together, it made a lot of sense to me. I realized that by working on just the mental aspect of this and not including the emotional, I was the one doubling the workload. If I could work on both of them simultaneously, I believed I would increase my capacity to recover.

I don't want to spend a lot of time discussing Sigmund Freud and his theories of emotional suppression and its link to trauma because it is a bit boring and there are conflicting thoughts on it, but let me recall some of what I found helpful.[30]

---

30 van der Kolk, Bessel, Dialogues in Clinical Neuroscience (2000) Mar; 2(1): 7–22. "Posttraumatic Stress Disorder and the Nature of Trauma." https://www.ncbi.nlm.nih.gov/pmc/articles/PMC3181584/

Freud believed there was a connection between a trauma that happened (brain) and the emotional response (heart) that someone experienced. If we have no way of discussing these traumatic occurrences when they happened to us (be it childhood abuse or things we saw or did during war), and if we do not have the resources, internal or external to deal with them, then we file them away for a later time. If these events are left unresolved, they will continue to bubble up and interfere with our day-to-day ability to function. So over time, we push them to the back of our mind into the body's long-term data retirement unit, the unconscious. This act of subduing or inhibiting these memories is called repression.

When repression takes place, Freud surmised that we are splitting the emotion of an event from the fact of the event. The fact and emotion, as we discussed, are filed under different recall mechanisms, and over time, the emotion becomes separated from the original fact. You may not remember why you feel uneasy in crowds, or you don't know why certain smells make you feel afraid, or why a car backfiring makes you throw yourself to the ground. These events *trigger* something in your unconscious and you respond emotionally, not logically. In fact, what I think is happening is that the body's systems are trying to put the mental memory back together with the heart memory so you can deal with it and understand it - *logically and emotionally.*

I believe this process also happens with self-sabotage. For example, you are thinking of starting a new business by yourself. Your mind memory is recalling the last time you started a business and it failed. It failed because your partner was a thief. Your heart is remembering feelings of failure. They might be feelings tied to other unrelated events, but it doesn't know that. You sit

there trying to make a decision about what to do; you're scared for whatever reason to start your business; and you don't know why. The ex-partner is in jail, so it's not logical you should be afraid, but you are. You are overcome with emotion because the event was traumatic for you. You lost your house and marriage because of it, and you have never really dealt with those issues. You just moved on. In reality, you didn't move on, you repressed it. What's happening now is the heart memory is trying to reconnect feelings and facts, but it can't. So the best it can do is warn you about anything it feels is related. Your heart is telling you that you shouldn't continue with this activity because last time you got hurt, and you'll get hurt again.

If you can find a way to take control of both of these potential negative forces - mind and emotion - and turn them around to be a positive force, then you'll leap ahead in recovery and not sink beneath the burden of it.

Therapy is a good place to start, but I don't believe it's the answer to everything. Freud said that the role of psychoanalysis was to try and help someone understand these emotions and in a sense re-attach them with the event that caused them. In other words, the job of a therapist is to help you with emotional detective work and bring about a level of self-awareness in someone. I believe that once you're aware of what the issues are - "I was abused," "I was blown up," "I screwed up because I am a selfish prick" – whatever it is, then the responsibility for your wholeness and wellness is yours.

Concluding rant

Did you notice that I said, "The responsibility for your wholeness and wellness is yours?" YOURS.

146

It isn't someone else's responsibility for you to get well.

If you take control of your mind, your desires and emotions, you take back control of your life. Your unconscious mind doesn't know the difference between visions of greatness or the longings of a loser. It just knows that you spend the majority of your time thinking about a particular thing in a particular way. It does not attach moral or ethical value to those things – *we do.*

<u>Leaving nothing in the ring</u>

I believe it takes everything you've got to become everything you want. Every ounce of discipline you can muster, every bit of determination to rise again when you fall is required to keep the end goal in sight. Lack of vision will drain a person of energy and vitality. I have often seen the most talented people become bored, restless, and sometimes physically sick because their minds are filled with nothing but petty problems and situations, worry, and stress. They don't have anything bigger to live for.

Most people are holdouts. Be it in the gym, in relationships, or in life; few people leave the field entirely spent. Results do not yield themselves to people who refuse to give themselves completely to their passions or dreams. When I coached boxing, so many people would try and save themselves for the next round; they were pacing themselves. But what if life doesn't give you the next round? What if the round you are currently in is the fight of your life? What if your entire future hinges on you having to win this one?

When I mentioned earlier that the average life span of one with BPD was 41 years, I wasn't quoting a stat. I was telling you about

147

one of the biggest wakeup calls I ever received. When I was first diagnosed and I read that figure, I was 45 years old. I was shocked, but encouraged, because I had beaten the odds. I was shocked because I realized I was living on statistically borrowed time.

If my writing or my story sounds like I am running downhill as fast as I can, it's because I am. This is my round; it could be my last round, and I don't want to leave anything in the ring.

Next steps

As I started to accept that all of this was true - that my mind and heart were connected and both needed A LOT of work, I knew I needed to make a plan on how to move forward. I couldn't work on all of it at once; but needed to identify a starting point that I could work on straightaway.

I found the best place to know what I needed to work on was to listen to myself speak because my words located me. If I found myself continually being negative in my view of myself, then that is where I would start. If my words were negative about my state of happiness, then I would work on that. I would take one thing at a time and focus on it.

If you get into a habit of listening to yourself speak and noticing the words that you say, you can identify the areas you need to develop with discipline in your life. This process is essential because your WORDS CREATE YOUR WORLD.

## ME AND MY SUPERPOWER

You are much stronger than you think you are. Trust me.

—Superman

The future is worth it. All the pain. All the tears. The future is worth the fight.

—Martian Manhunter

I remember early on when I was coming to terms with what happened to me that I got tired of talking about BPD/PTSD or my breakdown. I got sick of telling people about my past. So, in an attempt to become more positive, I made some vocabulary changes. I referred to PTS as an illness instead of a disorder. This term pissed some of my military mates off because they were trying very hard NOT to be seen as mentally ill, but as just having a disorder. I thought, *"Screw it, a disorder sounds like what crazy people say they have when they are trying to hide that they are crazy."* I can get better from an illness, or at least learn to manage it, but a disorder was something I was stuck with for life.

Around this time, my son Noah discovered comics and superheroes. One of my favorite memories is making up stories for him when he was young. He was always some super ninja warrior and always got the girl. Every night he would ask me to come and tell him a story. I regret the nights I said no – the nights when I was having a hard time standing in a dark room. I would do it differently now, but that's a moot point. I did the best I could with what I had and that is all you can ask of yourself.

Anyway, back to my superpower.

Growing up as a kid, I learned to get along with everybody to keep the peace. Out of sheer necessity, I taught myself to read body language as a survival skill. I read slight twitches in peoples' faces, noticed changes in voice pitch, and tension in areas of their body. I developed a *knowing* about certain people, an ability to read people, and how to read a room. I learned to identify a threat or the silent leader. Later in life, these became useful skills. Friends would often comment on my uncanny ability and insight.

After the recall in 2008, these skills or intuitions seemed to intensify. It's like the overlaying of the hyperactive areas of the brain, or the reluctance of the underactive areas to get involved, magnified these survival instincts. I remember one situation very clearly. I had just formed a partnership with friends, and we were looking at taking on a new contract for a corporate consultancy job. We went to a meeting with the prospective clients and blew them away. Everything went well – they were astounded at what we could do and excited about our input. Then right at the end of the meeting, a single comment was made with a name mentioned by the woman chairing the meeting. It's hard to explain, but something immediately got my attention, like a flash. I saw it, but before I could focus on it, it was gone; yet, I *knew* I had seen it. It wasn't the comment, but the slight change in voice, a shift in her body position, and how she adjusted her skirt. When we were debriefing as a team later, I shared what I had seen and what I thought it meant. My partners thought we should be celebrating when I knew differently.

I didn't handle myself very well during the Debrief. I had been triggered somehow and was heightened emotionally and verbally. I tried to communicate my concerns. My response to the team seemed way over the top and illogical. But I wouldn't be moved.

I was adamant the chairwoman was lying and the deal wasn't ours. I predicted that she'd take our proposal and repurpose it for her committee. I went on to tell my friends that I believed the person she would give the contract to would be the individual she mentioned in passing. My partners accused me of being negative, a "Debbie Downer," afraid of success, etc., but I wouldn't change my mind. I don't know how I knew, but I just knew. My knowing wasn't just based on what I saw. It was the overwhelming sense of fear and anxiety that washed over me as I picked up subtle changes in the faces of the people in the room.

Two weeks later, exactly what I said would play out played out, and the team couldn't believe it. "Dude, how did you do that? How did you know? Have you got some superpower?" I started to reflect on the times in my life when I just *knew* something. I recounted times when I hadn't listened to my superpower, and how things and relationships didn't go as smoothly as they should or could have. It would be years before I understood that the fruit of the changes in my brain were a gift and not a curse; however, from that day forward, I started referring to PTSD as my *superpower*.

## STRESS TO STRENGTH

Fire is the test of Gold. Adversity of Strong men.

—Seneca

Up to this point in my life, I never really saw myself as a creative person. I had written some books and journaled for years, but never really saw myself as a writer or as a poet. That perspective changed during the brief return trip to Australia. I don't know what started it. Maybe it was tied to the attempt of Fred and Rosemary to groom my son for abuse - maybe that was the trigger. All I know is that when it started, it didn't stop. I would sit for hours, while my family slept, and write and rewrite accounts and reflections on my childhood - all in poetic form.

The relief and release I felt when I wrote were incredible. For the first time, I was able to give voice to these experiences in a way that was different than just yelling them. The poetry wasn't "here is a lovely butterfly floating on a sunset" type of poetry. Most were dark, somewhat introspective works. Put it this way, with poems entitled:

- *The Wolf and the Whore* (the effects of sexual abuse on sexuality);
- *Cunts* (the impact of pornography on boys as they grow to men);
- *Soiled* (what it feels like after being abused); and
- *First Kiss* (an account of molestation by scout leaders)

I don't think you could call the final published work, *No Working Title*,[31] a coffee table book.

It also has other less dark, lighter poems:

- *Lion Taming* (a boy, his dog, and his imagination);
- *A Good Woman* (about my wife);
- *Psalm For The Broken* (a prayer for the abused); and
- *This Too Shall Pass* (vision for the future)

The point I'm trying to make is that I never wrote poetry before. Even after amassing a following of several hundred thousand readers/followers on social media, I never called myself a poet or saw myself as a poet. I was just a guy who wrote some stuff and hoped it helped people. So imagine how it felt when out of the blue, nine years after all of this started, I got an unsolicited email from Dr. Jeri Danielle Walker-Boone. Dr. Walker-Boone is an established poet. Her work has been included in over 50 published anthologies along with two books. She wrote:

*Dr. King,*

*You are, undoubtedly, one of the finest, most genuine, most vivacious and creative poets of this century. You dare to pen poems on extremely controvertible subjects and do so with flair and panache. CONGRATULATIONS!*

*- Dr. Jeri Danielle Walker-Boone*

---

31 http://www.drjohnaking.com/product/no-working-title-hardcover-poetry-book/

When asked about me, Melissa always told people I was a poet and a writer. I received emails thanking me for my work before but never something from an established fellow poet. It made me think, *"How does that work? How does that fit with my view of who I am? How do I go from an ex-rugby player and boxer to 'undoubtedly, one of the finest, most vivacious and creative poets of this century?'"*

The radically different way people saw me, compared to how I saw myself, struck me as odd. I started to wonder if the trauma and the changes to the brain had brought about other fundamental changes that I had yet to acknowledge or even recognize.

Let me outline briefly what the traditional thought has been concerning brain use and some new discussions that are emerging as a result of technology:

- Once a brain is damaged, it can never recover.
- We only use 10% of our brain's capacity, that's why we can never be as smart as other people because some people have genetically been given access to a larger percentage of their brain than the rest of us.
- Traditional thought for years is that the left side of the brain could be called the technical aspect of the brain. It handles planning, logic and critical thinking. The right side is like its hippie cousin. It is the creative, emotional, impulsive and intuitive side. If the left side is damaged, you are no longer able to perform these tasks efficiently and vice versa.

Let's discuss each of these traditional views on brain function in light of recent developments.

## Once damaged always damaged

Jacinta O'Shea[32] reported in 2007 how a backup brain region springs into action to compensate for disruption of a primary functional area. Researchers from Garvan Institute and UCLA[33] reported in 2013 that when the brain's primary learning center is damaged, complex new neural circuits arise to compensate for the lost function by creating alternate pathways - often far from the damaged site. For example, in the case of Alzheimer's or a stroke, the prefrontal cortex takes over when the hippocampus, the brain's key center of learning and memory formation, is disabled. The study showed that rats with a damaged hippocampus were able to learn new tasks. It took them a little longer to be trained, but they learned from their experience. One of the head guys in the project, Michael Fanselow said:

"The brain is heavily interconnected — you can get from any neuron in the brain to any other neuron via about six synaptic connections ... So there are many alternate pathways the brain can use, but it normally doesn't use them unless it's forced to. Once we understand how the brain makes these decisions, then we're in a position to encourage pathways to take over when they need to, especially in the case of brain damage."

## 10% theory is bogus

Barry Gordon at Johns Hopkins School of Medicine put it this way: "It turns out, that we use virtually every part of the brain, and that [most of] the brain is active almost all the time ... the

---

32 May 3, 2007 issue of the journal Neuron, published by Cell Press.

33 http://newsroom.ucla.edu/releases/brain-re-wires-itself-after-damage-246049

brain represents three percent of the body's weight and uses 20 percent of the body's energy."[34]

This misconception probably stems from people's need to justify why others are smarter than they are, and why they can do more in life. I'm not ruling out DNA or IQ, but it has nothing to do feeling you have a doughnut-sized brain like Homer Simpson.

## Left vs. Right

This issue or concept of the two halves of the same brain doing separate tasks with a sense of independence from each other or in competition with each other is a little bit like the Twix commercials; it tends to make a big to-do about nothing. Kosslyn and Miller[35] believe it is no longer left vs. right, but top vs. bottom. From a layman's point of view, this is semantics. My takeaway is that there are different regions in our brain with very different functions, but they work in full concert and awareness of each other. It's an entire organic system.

## Stress to Strength

What if my post-traumatic stress ended up being some sort of post-traumatic strength? What if somehow my brain, by having to rewire itself using the right side of my head to compensate for injuries on the left side, had tapped into something far more creative than I ever imagined?

---

34 https://www.scientificamerican.com/article/do-people-only-use-10-percent-of-their-brains/

35 http://ideas.time.com/2013/11/29/there-is-no-left-brainright-brain-divide/

We have all read about people who have had near death experiences, and how they talk about how their outlook on life changed; how they found new purpose and direction; how they focused on what was important to them in life and how life often took a new direction. I'm thinking *near death* is kinda up there on the list of all things traumatic.

In his book *Genius, Grief and Grace,*[36] Dr. Gaius Davies looks at some of the great leaders, humanitarian and creative talents of our times. He noted how their anxiety, guilt, depression, and traumatic life events all forged in them strength and perseverance. And in most cases, trauma birthed a talent that they would never have refined otherwise. It also gave them incredible compassion and insight into the human condition.

What if trauma, instead of being seen as a shitty experience, could be considered a fertilizing experience? What if somehow, like Marie Foregeard[37] had suggested, my creativity was a manifestation of growth, not stress? What if the difficulty I had come through, and the things I was wrestling with, had led me to develop and grow in new areas? What if I had to stop trying to reclaim the old John? What if he was gone forever? What if I would never be the man I once was? Did this give me hope that I could be someone new? Possibly even someone better?

---

36 Davies, Dr. Gaius, "Genius, Grief & Grace: A Doctor Looks as Suffering and Success." 2008, Christian Focus.

37 Forgeard, Marie J. C., "Perceiving benefits after adversity: The relationship between self-reported posttraumatic growth and creativity." Psychology of Aesthetics, Creativity, and the Arts, Vol 7(3), Aug 2013, 245-264.

Here I was, and for the first time in my life, all I wanted to do was sneak away to a beach somewhere and write poetry or books that would inspire people to do great and awesome things despite the trauma and tragedy they experienced in their lives. *Did I just want to escape or was this a NEW ME that was starting to emerge?*

## MEL'S TURN

John's ability to read a room is a real thing. I've seen it happen, and I was there in the business meeting he described. He was triggered when we debriefed; he came across so angry. Angry but also sure that what he said was going to happen would indeed happen. At the time, I thought he was just being unnecessarily negative, but then I tend to fall into the other Pollyanna-esque ditch when it comes to these things. You know, everyone is nice and no one is out to get you. This occasion was only one example — I've seen John do this over and over again in business meetings, coaching sessions, and even with his kids. What I'm learning to do is look past the sometimes-angry delivery and try to actually hear what he's saying, because it is a superpower indeed.

I've been intrigued with brain science since my early twenties, when my grandfather died from Alzheimer's complications. I'm certainly no doctor, but I believe there are so many things we don't yet know about the brain's ability to recover from, or work around, trauma. We are so fortunate to have walking miracles that we can learn from — like John and his veteran friends, and countless others, which is extremely exciting for the generations to come. Do I prefer that no one ever suffer trauma or contract Parkison's or Alzheimer's? Yes, but for the ones who do, I believe we will have better answers in just a few short years.

CHAPTER FIVE

# The Tale of Two Men

It is not the critic who counts; not the man who points out how the strong man stumbles, or where the doer of deeds could have done them better.

The credit belongs to the man who is actually in the arena, whose face is marred by dust and sweat and blood; who strives valiantly; who errs, who comes short again and again.

—President Theodore Roosevelt, *1910 Citizen of the Republic*

The thing that haunted me.

The thing that haunted me since John-A-Geddon was one of those silly can-never-be-answered questions I would wonder about for my ex-wife, my kids, and now Melissa.

Who could I have been if these things hadn't happened to me? What sort of man could I or would I have been for those I love?

How different would life have been for my first wife and kids if I hadn't been abused? Would my marriage have survived? How about my church or career or my business? What about Mel? She certainly wouldn't be trying to help me hold my life together with duct tape and wire; she would be probably off dancing the light fantastic with some other guy (lucky bastard).

*Most days I felt like a shadow of the man I might have been.*

I can remember who I was, and I wasn't that man anymore. I can remember how I used to work, behave in crowds, and rise every day with a sense of excitement about life. But I couldn't do that anymore. It became harder for me to understand things than it used to. It was difficult to grasp new concepts and complete tasks. I got lost easily because I couldn't remember or understand the directions I was given.

I always felt frustrated because things that were once easy to do or remember were now difficult. I'd look back at my 30-year-old self and wonder what happened to him. Surely years of experience and acquired knowledge were supposed to be working in my favor? I was supposed to be building on all that foundation instead of feeling like I was slowly declining.

I would reach for concepts in my mind or skills, things that I remember learning, but couldn't apply them or fully recall them for some reason. Previously performed tasks I had performed hundreds if not thousands of times before, were now a struggle to complete. I either simply couldn't do them, or my competency

# SHADOW OF A MAN

It is not the battle that concerns me

It's not the obstacles that must be met that keep me up at night

It's not the unknown that daunts me

It's not fear of failure....I've failed many times before... and like an old boxer, begged for one more round.

It is the sick feeling that I am

A shadow

Of what I could have been.

Taken from *No Working Title: a Life in Progress* by Dr. John A. King, available at www.drjohnaking.com.

level was nearly non-existent. Things I used to like, I now couldn't stand. Things I used to find challenging, I now enjoyed. I kept reaching for the old part of me, and it just wasn't there anymore.

People would tell me it was just old age, but that never sat well with me. When speaking with some of my ex-military mates, men much younger than I, they all talked about the same issues. It's not our bodies that are breaking down; we can still push those. It's our minds that concern us - they're broken, and we're just not the men we use to be. Literally. Those men were gone and would never be back.

Have you heard of phantom limbs? A phantom limb is a sensation reported by 60-80% of people who had a limb amputated. After the limb is removed, they still have the sensation or the memory of the limb being there. At times the limb felt painful, itched, and they would try to use their limb only to realize it wasn't there anymore. What they used to do, what they remember doing; they couldn't anymore. That is how I felt.

This set of phantom abilities is tough to come to terms with and accept, especially when as a man, all your self-esteem, your sense of self-worth is tied up in your ability to *do something.* I was a successful corporate coach and trainer. I was known for my ability to speak and inspire. I had a reputation for being self-confident, sanguine, a creative thinker, and a problem solver. It's not that I couldn't do those things anymore; it's just that I couldn't do them like I remember myself being able to do them. They would take so much more time, and to be honest, I didn't enjoy them as much anymore. I stumbled mentally. I stuttered whenever I was under emotional stress (which was all the time it seemed), and I didn't have a filter anymore. When I spoke to people, regardless

of the setting, I came across like the barkeeper with Tourette's in *Boondock Saints*. But I didn't have Tourette's, I just had a dose of "I'm fresh out of give-a-fucks."

<u>John 2.0</u>

Mel loves home shows - any and all of them. You know the ones where people see three houses, walk around, bitch and whine, and finally end up spending too much money? She sits there and argues with the TV the entire time. I get scared when she watches the home renovation ones because from experience I know they will inspire her. I'll come home one day and find some obscure piece of crap hanging above my bed that looks like lawn art from the 1970's, which I'm convinced will fall off the wall and decapitate me in my sleep.

Over lunch one day, we were watching this quirky British show about couples that were designing and building new homes or renovating old ones. This particular episode featured a British soldier who had lost three of his limbs in Afghanistan when he stepped on an IED. As you can imagine, this was a life-changing event for Captain Jon White and his wife, Becky. Overnight Jon had become a different man, mentally and physically. The things he could once do, he could still do, but he had to learn how to do them in a new, different and efficient way. Everything was new for them as a couple because Jon was a different man.

One of the things that Mel and I found most encouraging in watching the show was how Jon and Becky gave themselves permission to adapt their lives and their environment to themselves so they could live comfortably and productively. The adaptations were not based upon external approval or acceptance, but internal need

and the limitation and challenges that they both faced because of Jon's injuries and disabilities. The one that made me cry was the shower. Jon had no legs below the knees. They would have to shower together because Jon couldn't reach the taps or shower-head, he would have to sit on the floor. In the new house, they had completely redesigned the shower, unlike any other. Jon was now able to stand at the same level as his wife and could shower with her or by himself. Here was this couple redefining life not based on who he once was, but who he is now.

I realized I was my version of a Jon White standing in a shower repeatedly jumping for the taps and being frustrated every day that I couldn't reach them, which needed to stop. I realized if I didn't have legs, there would be no point bitching about how I couldn't reach the cookies on the top of the refrigerator. I would get a ladder, ask for help, or not have cookies. None of these scenarios would make me less of a man. I realized that I never gave myself permission to come to terms with how I was now different (and would always be different) than I was before. As a man and as a couple, Mel and I would have to learn to do love and life differently, if we were going to enjoy it.

Where to begin?

Building on the old wasn't going to work because I felt like the foundations were shaky. I was going through a period where I would attempt to do something the way I did it before and about 70% of the time it would fail. Things became confusing for me very quickly. Too many choices paralyzed me. Even small changes to established plans or arrangements would leave me spinning. I was struggling with being happy, in finding joy in what I was doing, and who I was.

I wouldn't say I was depressed; I just wasn't emotionally engaging with anyone or anything anymore. I felt like I lacked purpose and direction. Things that used to interest me didn't anymore; nor was I capable of doing them anyway. I found it difficult to concentrate at work, often because of lack of sleep, but mostly because I didn't care like I used to. I'd rather sit and write poetry, or fly a plane - those things would engage me and keep my mind occupied. Mona's parting advice to me, "John you have to get out of your head, it's a mess in there!" would prove to be very well founded.

One of our closest friends is a process engineer for one of the largest companies in the world. She is the Senior Vice President of Everything Someone Else Doesn't Want To Do. Her advice to me was, "When in doubt, make a list," so that's what I did. What I discovered was that the majority of what was on my list had to do with how I thought about myself and others, the world, and the past. If this issue were "all in my head," then with my head I would begin. This simple exercise not only confirmed the epiphany I had after the infamous sailing debacle, but it also gave me the next steps I needed in order to change the way I thought about myself and my life.

I had hundreds and hundreds of books in my study. Books I studied, read, and loved. These books provided me with the information I needed to get to where I was before, so logically they were a good place to start. I picked out my favorite ones that had coffee stains and markings all over them and bought new copies. I didn't want to see what was important to me before. I wanted to read the information with new eyes - hopefully wiser eyes. I was no longer a man with dis-abilities but one with CHANGED-ABILITIES. The prospect excited me; I felt like I was on a journey of discovery. It

is important that you notice I didn't say *re-discovery*. I wasn't doing a renovation, I was trying to get a blueprint to build a new life I would inhabit with my wife.

## YOU ARE NOT A BEAUTIFUL OR UNIQUE SNOWFLAKE

Perseverance always outlasts persecution.

—Me (a fortune cookie in China Town, San Francisco)

John Wick is a man of focus, commitment, sheer will.

—Viggo Tarasov

You are not special. You are not a beautiful or unique snowflake.

—Tyler Durden

**Perseverance:** dedication, stamina, tenacity[38]

**Persecution:** mistreatment, ill-treatment, oppression[39]

I started out by reading a lot of biographies. The people I read about were from varied backgrounds with some dating back to the early 1st and 2nd centuries. Most were from the 1800's and 1900's, while some were from the modern era. Some were theologians, medical doctors or scientists; others were sports or political figures. Everything from Lewis and Clark to Miyamoto Musashi - I read probably 100 biographies. As I read and re-read the lives of the people who had inspired me, I realized there was no secret to their success.

All these amazing folks who overcame seemingly insurmountable odds all shared a simple common belief: CONTINUE TO PUSH

---

38 http://www.thesaurus.com/browse/perseverance

39 http://www.thesaurus.com/browse/persecution?s=t

FORWARD BEYOND CIRCUMSTANCES OR DISABILITIES RELENTLESSLY AND LIVE A LIFE OF ACHIEVEMENT AND PERSONAL IMPACT. Each was committed to living full lives despite what others saw as setbacks. In other words, they simply found reasons to succeed and not excuses to fail or give up. I became firmly convinced that our lives are 10% what happens to us and 90% how we respond to it.

Years ago, I wrote down a quote from Ted Engstrom[40]:

> *"Cripple him, and you have a Sir Walter Scott. Lock him in a prison cell, and you have a John Bunyan. Bury him in the snows of Valley Forge, and you have a George Washington. Raise him in abject poverty, and you have an Abraham Lincoln. Subject him to bitter religious prejudice, and you have a Benjamin Disraeli. Strike him down with infantile paralysis, and he becomes Franklin D. Roosevelt. Call him a slow learner, 'retarded,' and write him off as uneducated, and you have an Albert Einstein."*

*Scott. Bunyan. Washington. Lincoln. Disraeli. Roosevelt. Einstein.* These men were not victims and refused to be crybabies. They refused to succumb to paranoia, or become cultural or ethnic victims. If you read even a brief Wikipedia-type biography of any of them, you will see that they had anything but an easy run at life. Some were from wealthy backgrounds, some were highly educated, but others were not. Some grew up as part of persecuted minorities, some born into dirt-floor poverty. All of them, however, seemed to possess indomitable hearts and an

---

40 Manser, Martin H. "The Westminster Collection of Christian Quotations," 2001. Westminster John Knox Press.

attitude that allowed them to march on regardless of whatever life threw at them.

Let's make this very, very clear: *life is not fair and sometimes what you face, what you go through, what happens to you is just plain wrong, even criminal.* BUT YOU'RE NOT SPECIAL OR UNIQUE. The world is not plotting against you; it's rough for everyone. Problems and pain exist. They will always exist, but they must never be allowed to conquer your soul.

At probably the lowest point in my life, a member of the Back Deck Crew (you'll learn more about them later) said, "John, you're in a hole, but for some reason you just keep digging. I would suggest that before you try to start climbing out, you throw the bloody shovel out so you're not tempted to dig any deeper." She made a good point.

You may not like to hear this, but shit doesn't always turn into fertilizer, sometimes it is just shit. You can stand there and try to sprout a flower, or you can climb out of the hole, have a shower, and move on.

<u>A survey of leaders</u>

As part of the leadership training programs I used to run, I would ask my attendees at the beginning of the day two simple questions. Hoping it would force them to be honest, I would only give them 5 minutes to write an answer.

The questions were:

- What is the one thing you want to achieve in your life - the thing you want to spend the rest of your days doing?
- What are three reasons you are not doing it, or three things that are keeping you back from your dream?

What always surprised me was that the answers, regardless of the group, were pretty much always the same.

No one I asked said they didn't have the ability to do what they wanted (except some idiot who was tone deaf and wanted to be an opera singer). Not one of them said they didn't believe they had the capacity to do what they wanted. No one blamed the economy or his or her ethnicity.

Here are the reasons they gave for not pursuing their passions in life:

- Lack of personal discipline
- Living in the past
- Not wanting it, just pretending to
- Fear of success
- Wasting time
- Procrastination
- Low self-esteem
- Lack of knowledge
- Fear of failure
- Lack of preparation
- Fear of what others might think

Each one of these people KNEW what it was they were supposed to do. They also knew that the one thing standing between them and their lifetime goals and ambitions were themselves. They

seemed to intuitively know their way of thinking was the greatest limitation to them obtaining their goals.

That is how I saw myself. I knew what I thought about myself, my life, and my future was inhibiting the ability to take my shower and move on. If you stay in the shit long enough you not only get used to the smell, but you also come to expect and anticipate it. The funny thing though, is once we move on we can at times long for the comfort of the smell, because it was familiar and safe. As a victim, having an excuse is always easier and less demanding that rebuilding from scratch.

## THOUGHTS ARE THINGS

Thinking is like loving and dying. Each of us must do it for himself.

—Josiah Royce

I understood the principle of *what is in you, comes out of you.* I could see the actual state of my head and my heart just by listening to how I was speaking. My words were locating me and I had to deal with what I heard coming out of my mouth. I know it sounds like a gift shop bookmark, but it was vital for me. Life was so stinking bad. Every day was a nightmare of self-doubt, self-judgment, fear, panic and a total, overwhelming sense of failure. It totally sucked. If I didn't change what was in me, there was no way I could change what came out of me; and consequently, I would never change the fruit of my life.

I didn't know where I was going or what the future would hold. I didn't even know what the new version of me was going to be. I just knew I didn't want to be here. I didn't want to be this version of me anymore. I needed to change what was in my head and my heart.

I was listening to an old sales recording by a guy called Earl Nightingale and from his talk to his sales guys came two reflections that became the foundation for my growth and development going forward:

- You become what you think about.
- You have to pay the price for anything of value.

<u>You have to sow good seed into good soil</u>

My first degree is in Agriculture. I put myself through college driving trucks and mustering cattle in outback New South Wales, Australia. On the farms, we would sow various crops at various times of the year - often oats in the spring and wheat in the summer.

At planting time, you never wanted to get your grains mixed up. If you had more than a certain percentage of the wrong crop mixed in with your harvest; for example, oats mixed in with your wheat harvest, the harvest was deemed contaminated, and you wouldn't receive the maximum price from the grain buyers.

I remember I was working in a little bush town called Trangie for a guy named Rob, and it was sowing season. We had a bunch of rain, and he had the best land in the district. My job was to drive a tractor that pulled a 48-foot sowing implement behind it. The sower was a disc plough with a seed bin on top and sowing tines with seed tubes attached. The disc broke up the soil and gravity fed the tubes that placed the seed in the ground - you get the idea.

While sowing, I noticed that we weren't using anywhere near enough seed for the size of the field. I talked to Rob because I wanted to check the sower, but was told that I was the college kid, to shut up and leave it to the grownups; everything was fine.

When the harvest came up there was a single line of wheat that went around and around in circles, following the path I had sown. You see, Rob was a lazy bastard and hadn't checked his equipment before he set me to work in that field. We were in the middle of a mouse plague, and every night, tens of thousands of mice would swarm the town looking for food. Where was the best

place to find it? In the seed bins and feeder tubes on the sowing equipment. When we pulled the tubes off the equipment, all but one of them were jammed with hundreds of mice that had died in a frenzy, eating the seed and were unable to get back out.

If a farmer doesn't pay attention to the proper care and maintenance of his equipment, if he didn't clean it out properly after each use, or if he mingles the wrong seeds, what he ended up reaping was not what he had hoped for or planned to reap.

Let's assume the farmer has a good block of land that's well irrigated with fertile soil, and the land has a proven potential based on past results. If these things are in place, then the land guarantees the farmer two things:

- Whatever the farmer puts into the land will grow, and he'll reap a harvest.
- Based on the quality of the seed and the farmer's care for the crop, his return could be 30, 60 or 100 percent.

The farmer's return doesn't depend on the land, soil, or amount of water available; all of those are constant. The land is neutral. The land cannot tell the difference between the seeds sown. The land doesn't know if it's oats, wheat, or weeds. The land doesn't know if it's getting enough water or not; it'll just use whatever it has in the way that it can. The land will treat the seeds the same; it will give each seed an opportunity to grow to its fullest potential.

The harvest is based solely on the farmer's attitude and attention to detail. The only time you'll judge how the farmer cared for his land and his crop will be at harvest time.

Let's look at it another way. The farmer digs two holes and plants two seeds: one oats and one wheat. He then covers them up, and he waters them both. The land will do what the land was designed to do; it will produce and bring forth fruit according to the seed planted. Now, imagine that the farmer planted both seeds in his field with full knowledge that half his crop is oats and the other half is wheat.

The farmer can wish the oats do not sprout. He can hope for only wheat to grow and be ripe for harvest. He can pray for his crop all that he wants, but the fate of the crop is already sealed because the seed will produce after its kind. Once the seed is planted and watered, unless the sprouting plant is forcefully and deliberately removed, it will bear fruit. The fruit will be according to the seed (after nature and after the character of the seed).

What Earl Nightingale suggested was that the human mind was far more fertile ground with far greater potential than any plot of land. He suggested, however, that it worked in the same manner: what you sow into the field of your mind will produce a physical crop in your life.

Another way of saying this: YOU BECOME WHAT YOU THINK ABOUT, OR THOUGHTS ARE THINGS.

When I heard this, I had an overwhelming desire to call bullshit and call it a bunch of tree-hugger, new-age crap. Why? It sounded too easy.

So there I am, over coffee, trying to discredit Nightingale and come up with a much more complicated self-development path,

when I started reading the business section of the USA Today. I noticed two juxtaposed articles about two groups of people.

The first article was about two unemployed brothers (Group 1). They had just won a million dollars from a Super Bowl advertisement they created on their home computer for about $200.

The second article was about three different sets of people (Group 2): two couples and one single woman. All were fearful and concerned about their future due to the condition of the economy, uncertain jobs, and the war overseas. The article described how these three sets of successful, professional people were selling their houses and moving back in with their parents, just in case something bad happened to them economically.

And it struck me: Bugger, that crafty bastard Nightingale was right! Same paper, same day, same economy, two groups of people - both about the same age, same demographic, and similar education - with the only difference being their mindset. In a sense, Group 1 and 2 had the same opportunities presented to them - their *land* was the same. But the difference in outlook and outcome was undeniable, and it all came down to one small thing - they each became what they were thinking about.

Both groups were filling their heads and their hearts with different seeds, and they were going to reap different crops for their lives. The two brothers dreamed big and won big. They swung for the fences. They realized the worst that could happen is they'd lose $200, and the best that could happen would change their lives forever. The other group who sold their houses and moved in with their parents lost out big time and probably set a pattern for the rest of their lives.

*Elephant Feet[41]*

## Elephant on a chain - the power of personal history

If you've ever travelled through Asia, you've probably seen big, old elephants just standing in the middle of a crowded square, chained to a little stake by a tiny chain. I've looked at the size of the chain and then the size of the elephant and always wondered: Why doesn't the elephant just run off? Why does it just stand there, walking in circles around that little stake all day long? That's not what elephants were destined or designed to do. What has happened to the wild, unfettered greatness that lies within its DNA? Why does it act like that? Why?

---

41 Sini Merikallio, Elephant Feet. 2012, Digital Image. Available from: Flickr, https://www.flickr.com/photos/smerikal/7634930564 (accessed January 20, 2017).

If you talk to the trainers and village people the answer is depressingly simple: it's because that is all the elephant has ever known. That is all the magnificent beast has come to expect from life. When the elephant was young, the villagers would drive a stake into the ground and chain the young elephant there. No matter how hard the baby elephant pulled and struggled, it couldn't move the stake. No matter how hard it rubbed against the iron ring, it couldn't get it off its leg. That elephant grows up expecting, believing, and experiencing the bondage of that chain. It never realizes that its strength and ability to remove that chain has changed over time. It doesn't understand that if it just decided to run for it, it would be free.

We are like that. We grow up a certain way. We are taught a certain thing. We are told that what we have and have experienced is all we can expect from life. We never bother to test the chains and the stakes that make up that narrative. The worse thing is when we start empowering the chain and stake by speaking to the chain and telling it how it is holding us back and how it is responsible for the limitations and voids we are experiencing. I'd go so far as to say that people hand over their potential to the chain and stake that bind them. They refuse to see the possibility of life without the bonds of culture, fear, poverty or sickness, abuse, illness, etc. They consign themselves to a hopeless, restricted future. Many spend their whole lives without really flexing their muscles and re-envisioning who they are, based on the REAL potential that lies within them.

The elephant never thinks about freedom; the elephant only thinks about the chain. It's so focused on what it has never been able to do before, that it never tests boundaries or tries something different. We can be like that. Dr. Edward Miller, dean of the medical school

and CEO of the hospital at Johns Hopkins University, made this incredible statement:[42]

"If you look at people after coronary-artery bypass grafting two years later, 90% of them have not changed their lifestyle... "

These patients, regardless that their lives were at risk, stayed chained to old paradigms, doing the same things and getting the same results and committing death by fast-food one supersize hamburger with fries at a time.

<u>You value what you pay for</u>

As I mentioned, the second thing I came to understand from old Earl Nightingale was that people only really valued what they paid for. The money and effort they had to give to obtain something are why they spent so much time hovering over it, looking after it, or showing it off. They will value a house, a car, a book, or an outfit because they had to pay for them.

The things we do not pay for we do not seem to value so highly. You cannot replace a friendship. You cannot replace a marriage. You cannot replace time. You cannot replace your health. You cannot replace your mind. You cannot replace an opportunity. We seem to treat these things with little or no regard even to the point of contempt. We paid nothing for them; therefore, we tend to put little value on them until they're gone, and we take them for granted.

---

42 Deutschman, Alan, "Change or Die." Fast Company, May 2005. https:// www.fastcompany.com/52717/change-or-die

I knew this to be true in my own life. I stand rightly accused of letting what was valuable to me slip away. I could continue to blame the chain or take responsibility for my past. I believed that if I took responsibility for my past and my mistakes, it would qualify me to have responsibility for the development and possibility of my future.

During this process, I identified three *chains* that I needed to confront. I noticed when I talked about my past, I did so with such venom and bitterness that it affected my mood, outlook, and relationships. Who the hell wants to hang out with a misery guts, regardless of why he was a misery guts? I felt like it was all tied in together somehow. I felt guilty because of the turn my life had taken. I felt guilty for getting abused, because of the impact my PTSD-driven behavior was now having on people who I loved. I knew if I didn't break free from this, I'd never move on.

# THREE THINGS I NEEDED TO DEAL WITH

#### #1. Honor Your Father and Mother / Commandment #5 – *Ain't Going to Happen*

This one's a tough write.

Tough because people want to know how I dealt with this and most don't seem happy with how I did. Tough because I don't know if it will be helpful. Tough because I think I'll sound weak when I tell it. Maybe tough because I don't want to have to sit and think about this crap again and it is messy to tell.

It was and still is, a process. Every time I have a challenging day or I'm dealing with the consequences of my broken marriage and life, my immediate response toward Fred and Rosemary is: "I WANT TO FUCKING KILL YOU." When asked if I have family back in Australia, I say, "A sister, I am orphaned." If I talk about my parents I don't call them my parents. I call them Fred and Rosemary the people who raised me.

When the memories came back, I didn't confront Fred and Rosemary about them. I was in the U.S., and they were back in Australia. I don't know why I didn't. I suppose I wanted to believe that if I saw and talked to them again that they'd apologize, and we would mend as a family. I know that's hard for some to understand, but for so many years all I wanted was to be loved and accepted by them. I use to imagine them telling me they were proud of me, like they were my sister. I was in my mid-40's and still needing and wanting that affirmation. My inability to confront and break those ties put a further strain on my first marriage. We didn't have a lot of interaction with them outside of the occasional video

call, but the kids still had attachments to them and asked about them. My reluctance to deal with the situation, I am sure lead to my then-wife losing further respect for me. I was all about men protecting their families, and she probably felt I was leaving a door open to wolves.

One day we got a call from the State Department that my then-wife won the Green Card Lottery. The odds had been so high against us winning it, we were unprepared, and we had to leave within 14 days. Tickets were expensive and hotels and rental cars in Sydney were ridiculously priced. My then-wife didn't want me to tell Fred and Rosemary that we were coming. I made all sorts of excuses as to why we had to see them - how they could help us with cars and accommodation, money, etc. but deep down I was probably hoping for that apology.

*The things you hear over a beer*

I didn't tell Fred and Rosemary when we were coming in. I wanted to get the Green Card done, and I wanted to have a chat with my little sister, Mary. Life had been tough for her too. She had been in therapy for 20 years. She was beautiful and smart, but filled with self-loathing. I always imagined it was something akin to survivor's guilt. From my very first memory of abuse, there was always a choice involved and a decision I had to make, "We can do this to you or Mary. You can come with us, or we will take Mary, you decide." I always let them take me. Later in life, I would easily take the blame for any infraction, supposed or real, and suffer the consequences for it. I just wanted to protect my sister. I never talked about any of this with her until one Sunday afternoon when we got together at a rooftop beer garden overlooking Sydney Harbor.

As we sat and talked, I opened up to her about John-A-Geddon and all I had remembered. I went through story after story. Instead of being shocked, she was amazed. She said she remembered all that stuff, but thought she had made it up. She had been in therapy because of the *fake* memories. Then she started to fill in the other half of the story for me. She told me about other things that had happened that she remembered. That night I cried with relief. I felt like I had received confirmation that I wasn't crazy or delusional, and I hadn't made anything up.

The conversation with Mary forced me to realize I needed to confront my parents, but I still lacked the strength. For me it was all in the past; I didn't want to go over the stuff again. Sadly, I still craved and needed their affection and approval. *Another nail in the marriage coffin.* But then, they started after my boy.

It began subtly at a museum one day. My then-wife told me that Rosemary approached her and asked if Noah had a learning disability, then turned around and walked off. About 30 minutes later, she came back and asked her if we had ever tested him for autism and again went away. She came back a third time and took Noah for a little stroll to look at dinosaurs. We found them hidden in an alcove, and my son was crying. Grandma was in the middle of a rant about how all boys are stupid and useless and good for nothing and not necessary in the world, and Grandma would teach him how to be a good boy and how to make her and all the other women happy.

When confronted, Rosemary very cleverly and convincingly explained how we had misheard the conversation. She was a grandmother and grandmothers would never say something like that about little boys. She made a point of telling us how she had

raised me, and that she was a university scholar and prominent educator who knew how important it was to build young boys' confidence and that she would never do anything to hurt him. My then-wife took him away, and I stood paralyzed by a new set of memories of having been made to stand in front of my mothers' friends to justify my very existence.

I talked to my sister about what had happened, and she told me an identical story but with an additional twist. Every time Fred and Rosemary minded her children, she would come home, and her son would be angry and in tears. Rosemary would just brush it off as "little boys get like that." Then Mary noticed that when he was home and made a mistake or she corrected him for doing something wrong, he would start to scream things like, "I am useless. I'm rotten. I'm a fucking little retard!" He was 6. Then there was her daughter. Fred accused her of being a sexual pervert. He accused her of grinding her vagina up and down his leg using it to masturbate. She was 9. My sister all this time blamed herself. Maybe she was a bad mother? Maybe this was just a little girl's sexual inquiry? Maybe it was her marriage? But now we both were confronted with how Rosemary and Fred were actively grooming our children.

As I write this, I feel like such a wimp. I want to write it differently so you - the perfect stranger I will probably never meet - will think highly of me, but I can't. There was no grand gesture; no epic standoff. I wish my narrative was, "I confronted Fred, beat his arse, bitch-slapped Rosemary and dragged them to court," but it isn't. Instead, we packed up and moved about two hours outside of Sydney to my wife's parents' place to wait for the Embassy's decision on our Green Cards. I told Fred and Rosemary we had

left the country. I needed to protect my son, but I still couldn't bring myself to confront them.

As I write this, I realize that this tiny little stance, this BOLD move of slinking away, was the start of my journey out of my past. It was, as I sat on a little chair outside that 200 square foot cabin at night by the beach, when I started to write poetry. It was there that I penned my very first piece, "Rain." It was there that I probably started to heal by allowing myself to get healthfully angry as I had time to reflect on what I had learned and what had happened.

*A confrontation of sorts*

When we returned to the U.S., things continued to become increasingly painful. My mind was purging memories like puss from an infected wound whenever it randomly decided I needed to deal with something. Around this time, I was experiencing the worst sleep deprivation and was the most emotionally deregulated. It was the most destructive time in my interpersonal relationships.

One day I was sitting in my shed just pissed off. Pissed off at everything and pissed off at Fred and Rosemary. Pissed off that I didn't beat the shit out of Fred or slap Rosemary. I looked at Australian law and my options. There was no statute of limitations on abuse. I would have to fly back there, secure legal counsel and prepare for a long legal battle. My plan was to write Rosemary an email asking for answers to some of the not-so-damning incidents. Her response would act as a confession of sorts, and I could get her and Fred in court and bring into the light everything they had done.

Here are some of the 13 questions I asked:

- Why was I knowingly exposed to pornographic magazines at 5 and 6 years of age?
- Why was I taken to watch pornographic movies?
- Why did we always have to talk while you were naked in the bath?
- Why didn't you protect me from this?
- Why did you allow it?
- Why did I have to stand in front of your friends and justify my existence?

Her reply was one of those ridiculous, "I can neither confirm nor deny" responses. She never disputed these events took place; she just never admitted that they did. The letter overflowed with her love for me as a mother and how life and/or memories of events weren't perfect. How she and Fred grew up in poverty and how they did their best, and did I know they both had difficult childhoods? They turned out okay and would never have hurt me - I was their golden boy. She is a very smart woman and everything she said was designed to cover her butt legally.

I knew without some solid evidence, it would all come down to a he-said-she-said situation. I did not want to stand in court and have to live through all of this again, only to listen to them both rationalize, justify and ultimately deny what they did to me. I was self-aware enough to know the fickle nature of memories. I knew that under cross-examination the defense attorneys would aim to rattle me and even try to induce an episode to negate my testimony. I wasn't well enough to deal with all of that.

*Why I never pursued justice later on*

People often ask why I didn't pursue some legal justice, even if it were just a day in court to confront them.

Over the next few weeks, as I reflected on her reply, I realized that this sense of injustice was consuming me. I was becoming bitter and angry. It was magnifying my condition and not helping me in any way. I realized that this affliction was infecting me. It was the only thing I was thinking about. I came to accept that all my fixation was doing was continuing to give them power over me and my life, and I wanted that to stop once and for all.

So I made the simple decision that I would live forward, not back. That the best *justice* I could have was to live a full and happy life.

And yes, this is way easier to say than it is to do. I still battle it. Writing this makes me flare up with indignation as to what it has cost me and those I love. The injustice of it all and the feeling of helplessness are sometimes overwhelming. However, it is a decision I don't regret and won't go back on.

*The final step toward freedom, dealing with Commandment #5.*

Even if you're not a Jew or a Christian you probably grew up with this concept. Throughout this process, I battled with how do I deal with the biblical command to "honor your father and mother that you will live a long time and life will be good to you?"[43] I didn't know what that meant, but I was pretty sure imagining Fred and

---

43 This is my paraphrase of Exodus 20:12 and Deuteronomy 5:16.

Rosemary roasting over hot coals basted in a garlic sauce didn't satisfy the 5th commandment.

I was preaching one night when a lady came up to me and told me her story of abuse by her cousins as a child. Her mother knew and didn't do anything to stop it. At the end of her story, she said, "How do I honor my mother and father when they did that?" She didn't know my background. I sat there looking at her and was stumped. I couldn't help her because I couldn't answer it for myself.

I looked at this young lady and said, "I honestly don't know." I ended up telling her what was going on in my life; that I was struggling to answer that same question. I said we had to get past it somehow and that if we didn't, we would never move on in our lives. I asked her to give me a week, and I'd have something for us both. What I discovered would do us both lots of good, and I hope it helps some of you as well.

Originally the 5th commandment wasn't taught in Sunday school to cute kids in short pants or summer dresses. Moses gave it to the children of Israel with the aim of protecting an aging population from elder abuse. It was designed to protect parents[44] from being

---

44 Jesus dealt with the same issue during His lifetime. Mark 7:10-13

Barnes makes this observation in his commentary:

The law of God required that a son should honor his parent;

i.e., among other things, provide for his wants when he was old, and in distress.

Yet the Jewish teachers said that it was more important for a man to dedicate his property to God than to provide for the wants of his parent. If a parent was needy and poor, and if he should apply to a son for assistance, and the son should reply, though in anger, "It is devoted to God--- this property which you need,

driven out of the family home in their old age and being left to die when they could no longer work or provide for themselves.

In her book, Broken Tablets[45], Racheal Mikvah suggested the word *honor* is best defined as:

- Do not take your parents' place or position.
- Do not diminish the esteem that is due them in the eyes of others.

To honor my parents meant that I was not to compete with them. Not to compete for the affection of your father that belongs to your mother or vice versa. Don't get between them, don't try and cause a split between them. Don't compete with them regarding authority. When you enter under your father's roof, remember it is your father's roof. It is his home.

Got it, I can do that; I won't ever see them again.

Next...

Don't diminish them, don't lessen, don't weaken or make small who your parents are in the eyes of their friends, your relatives or even perfect strangers.

I could do that also.

---

and by which you might be profited by me, is corban, I give to God," the Jews said the property could not be recalled, and the son was not under obligation to aid a parent with it.

45 Mikvah, Rachel S. "Broken Tablets: Restoring the Ten Commandments and Ourselves," 2001. Jewish Lights.

The decision I made was to not speak negatively about them. I allowed myself to discuss the truth of my life and its experience in full. I just wouldn't engage in any conversation or communication that could anyway imply that I was not grateful for being born. To this day, when people ask me if I would change my past, I say no. It made me who I am today, and I am very grateful for my life. It's not a life I would wish on anyone else, but it is my life and my experiences. And I'm glad I was born.

It is hard to express what happened in that small moment. The best way to say it is I felt like the last chain of attachment was broken. I walked away from the stake of resentment that was holding me back. I felt free.

#2. Guilt vs. Conscience

I was reluctant to embrace the diagnosis of PTSD because I didn't want others to see me as playing the victim. I'm not saying that people with genuine PTSD play victims, in fact, the ones I know rarely talk about it. What pissed me off was every day it seemed some idiot was trying to take their pony or peacock on an airplane as an emotional support animal. They had decided that they were suffering some kind of trauma as a result of a cancelled hair appointment or a broken nail, and it was causing the rest of us to be stereotyped as narcissistic fools. I went so far as refusing to get a service dog vest for my dog because I didn't want to get lumped in with those morons.

But if PTSD was what I had, then I needed to come to terms with that and accept it, along with accepting that there were some consequences from the condition. These consequences affected

my behavior in the past and were things I needed to watch out for in my future.

My big one was that I felt guilty. Every day I was either reminding myself or was being reminded by someone that I had failed as a man, a husband, a father, a leader, and a Christian. These feelings of guilt weighed me down. I knew I had done and said things that were wrong. I wasn't trying to get a free pass. Every day I would own my mistakes, and with every error I made, I sincerely apologized and did everything I could to get it right the next time. But I was broken and I didn't yet possess the ability or skillset to cope with life as it came at me. The guilt was strangling my ability to move forward. I wasn't trying to get out of the consequences of my actions; I am not that guy. I just needed to find a way to come to terms with how I didn't go looking for this illness, this event, this past, whatever it was, it had come looking for me. As a result of this illness[46], I had done things, said things, and made decisions that I now had to live with. Life had taken an unexpected turn and was going in an unexpected direction. There was no going back. I had to move forward, but I couldn't do it weighed down with the excess baggage of the guilt of my mistakes.

---

46 Some folks object to my use of the term illness, they say it is a misdiagnosis and classification of PTSD. First of all, I don't care what they think. Secondly, I find it a lot easier to say, "I got sick, and my life fell apart because of it," than to say, "I've got a mental disorder called PTSD." All of a sudden, I'm lumped in with every whack job who has gone postal in the last 20 years.

That, my friends, is why many of our veterans refuse to talk about their conditions. People do not understand. They will not employ us, but want to sit around and ask stupid questions like, "Did you kill someone over there?" Or, "What was it like having sex with your mum?" We will let some crusading social worker battle that front for us while we go for a beer and mock support pigs.

I didn't struggle with a guilty conscience, that part was broken. I struggled with being condemned as guilty. I felt everyone I had ever known was judging me for not being a big enough man not to have allowed this neurological change to affect me. I spoke to a mate yesterday; last Sunday was Father's Day. He is a veteran who saw and did some crazy stuff. He ended up with PTSD, divorced, and estranged from his daughters. His girls didn't even call him on Father's day. One of my girls didn't call me. It was heartbreaking for us both. It's not that either of us wants or expects a free pass. It would just be nice for our girls or our exes or maybe even people who knew what we faced, to look at us and say, "I see you trying. I know things didn't work out, I know things got too bad for everyone, but I see you trying." But they don't, or can't, or won't.

I began to wonder how much of my life I had spent condemning myself for old crimes and old mistakes. And I asked myself how much of my life was I going to waste on fretting over "shoulda-been, coulda-been and woulda-been?"

Maybe my issue wasn't that I had made mistakes. Maybe it was that I was living condemned by the words, thoughts and opinions of other people when God himself wasn't holding things against me. Maybe what God values and what the people value just aren't the same things?

### #3. All women are lying, manipulative, betraying, abusive bitches that can't be trusted.

The title is deliberately deceptive. I have never thought that way. I don't know how or why, but I just never have.

It's 2:30 A.M., and I knew I had to write this piece today. I wanted to start by comparing my earliest memories to those of other kids. Then I realized that I was sitting here Googling "earliest childhood memories" to give you examples, and I am laughing at the absurdity of it. I have no idea what a normal childhood memory might be.

It's 4:20 A.M., and this makes me physically sick to recall, but I need to make my point.

My sister and I were placed at the end of my parent's bed, and we sat watching while "mummy and daddy played a game." The game was putting a mixture of bread, water and honey into Rosemary's vagina. How we got to join in was that one of us was going to be allowed to get it out of there with our tongues. I don't know how a 4-year-old knows this sort of thing, but I just knew it was not a *nice* thing to be doing, and I knew it was my job to look after my little sister. So I crawled forward on the sheets and buried my face between my mother's thighs while my father watched.

I remember it was one of the few times in my childhood my mother was physically affectionate towards me. Rosemary lovingly stroked my hair. Between soft groans of approval, she spoke to me in a way she had never spoken to me before. In a voice I can still hear to this day, "That's a good boy, you're doing such a good job, mummy loves you very much."

Later, when I was about 6 or 7 years old, I was in my parent's bed, under my mother's nightgown, and Fred walked in. Something was said between them, and clearly, he was no longer pleased by what I was doing. As he stormed out of the room, I remember

his look of pure hatred towards me. From that point on, things started to change between us.

Have you ever seen those movies set in the 1970's where there is a room full of lava lamps, people wearing polyester leisure suits all lying/sitting around on white shag-pile carpet bean bags, smoking joints? Those people were my parent's friends. They had come out of the free sex movement of the 60's, got married and decided monogamy was boring; so they had swinger parties. The men would throw their car keys into the middle of the circle, and the women would pick out a set of keys. Whoever owned the keys a woman picked, she went home with for the night. Or, if it were a stay-in party, they'd find a corner or a beanbag and have sex.

I remember one night my parents took me to one of those parties. In the lounge room they were smoking joints and playing the bongos, and I thought that was cool. This nice guy lets me sit with him, and he taught me to play. After a while, I wandered off into another room filled with people watching a porn film projected on the wall. I remember Rosemary introducing me to a fat lady lying on a beanbag wearing a kaftan and telling me to crawl under her dress and "make her tingle just like you make mummy."

I don't remember much else from that evening, except that there was some filming done on one of those old Kodak hand-held movie cameras. I know I was a part of the film, but I can't remember what part or what I was doing at the time.

As I grew older and started to develop as a young man, the nature of what I experienced changed. I remember one particular occasion when my mother gathered a group of her friends in our home for what she called a "friendly debate." She was part of the feminist

academia at Macquarie University in Sydney. As they sat there on the sofa, I was invited into the room and made to stand before them. The topic they were discussing was the value and the role of men in society. As a group, they subscribed to the doctrine that men caused all evil in the world, and that all men are rapists and abusers and should be placed in a concentration camp.[47]

As they outlined their argument to me, they stated that men were no longer necessary in society, and they as feminists were committed to destroying the heterosexual family unit and all men in general. But they were going to give me a chance to redeem myself and all other men. I was allowed to debate with them on the issue. I think I was 13 at the time.

For an hour or so, I was forced to answer their questions. Based on my responses, they berated and belittled me and said all men are useless and all boys are mistakes. The limit of the contribution of men to society was the donation of our sperm to a sperm bank if we qualified. And we were not needed for anything else. The professor of feminist studies at the time said, "Why don't you do us all a favor and cut your dick off; we could make quite a nice little cunt out of it for you." Rosemary sat there laughing, applauding and encouraging the conversation.

*Why recount all of this?*

I write all of this down to make the simple point that the majority of abuse I suffered was at the hands of women: namely Rosemary,

---

[47] A doctrine restated by Julie Bindel in 2015 http://theothermccain. com/2015/09/06/guardian-columnist-julie-bindel-says-put-all-males-in-some-kind-of-camp/

her friends, Fred's girlfriends and women at their parties. If ever there were a man who had a right, and I do mean right, to be bitter and twisted in his view towards women because of experiences in his life, I am more than qualified. But I am not bitter or twisted, and I refuse to be. I refuse to lump the good women in my life and the world with the evil, perverted minority that I encountered. Mathematically, how could I say that all women are manipulative, self-seeking, abusive bitches when:

- I have not met all women; and
- The women who I now count as close to me are incredibly trustworthy and wonderful friends?

Over my lifetime, I have listened to people bitch and whine about the opposite gender and never thought it was helpful or healthy. Their attitudes seem to perpetuate The Victim Narrative and prohibit their ability to move forward in life. I have never understood how women or men who are married and have sons and daughters can allow themselves to continue to perpetuate an attitude that is so incredibly harmful to their relationships.

Why would you ever want your kids to hear you say, "All men/women are bastards/bitches?" Or, your husband/wife to believe that is what you think about them? I think this is the most prevalent and obvious case of the "victim becoming the abuser."

If I have a rough day concerning memories of abuse, or an encounter with women that reminds me of Rosemary or her friends - in other words, a trigger - I try to make sure I spend time remembering there are women in my life who are good women. They may be flawed, but they are wonderful; and they love and care for me. I don't want any anti-female sentiment to pervert or poison my

life. I won't allow these attitudes to seep down to my children. I want my girls to see themselves as valuable and to love and care for their husbands all their days. I want my son to be a strong man who will grow up to love and care for his wife all his days.

To perpetuate these negative gender-based victim stereotypes is harmful and detrimental to the little boys and girls like I was, who every day suffer because some grownup couldn't scrape their crap together in a pile and move on. I have not allowed my pain to blinker me to the needs of humanity, or to the needs of little girls or women. In fact, I have actively used it to encourage myself to keep my eyes open and aware of the needs of humanity. And, I strongly believe that sexual abuse is a human rights' issue; not a gender rights' issue.

He is 11, he is a naked boy.
Daddy watches him as the other men laugh at his hairless body. They take turns pulling his dick to make it grow. The pliers hurt the most.
Do you see him?

He is 13, he is a lonely boy.
The scouts leader says, "Let me hold it for you, thats how we become friends."
Do you see him?

He is 45, he is a screaming man.
Curled in a ball, sobbing body shuddering with memories that are shattering his soul and breaking his mind.
Do you see him?

He is 50, he is a broken man.
Nursing a bottle and sucking a barrel.
Do you see him?

He is 53, he is a relentless man.
His arse will always bleed and his eyes will never dry.
Do you see him?

He is a survivor too.

By Dr. John A. King, originally published at www.drjohnaking.com.

## MEL'S TURN

"The Tale of Two Men" is a tough read for me. I met John only a couple of months before John-A-Geddon, and we became friends over the next few years, so I didn't know much of John 1.0. I don't pretend to know what it would have been like for his first wife to watch the change take place - the man she married was suddenly no longer there.

What I do know is that John still deals with the dichotomy every day. When he sits down to work and can't seem to focus, he remembers how he used to execute like a machine. When he tries to write and can't seem to make the words match the picture in his head, he remembers how sentences used to flow so easily. He requires quiet spaces, which can be hard to achieve in our lovely, open-floor plan home. With the kids and the dog and me all moving around and doing our thing, it seems like interruptions (and the resulting frustration!) are inevitable. He wrote most of this book hunched over his workbench in the garage - with no air-conditioning... in July/August... in Texas.

I know John also struggles with what might happen to his brain as he gets older. Will it degenerate further? Is he at greater risk for Alzheimer's or Parkinson's or the ills associated with Traumatic Brain Injury? Science hasn't answered those questions yet, and he's left with a sense that his days are numbered. He worries about me. He shouldn't. I am happy to love him as much as I can for as long as we have. We will live hard and squeeze the most out of every day, doing the most good we can for everyone we meet.

Don't get me wrong, I have many, many, (TONS actually), selfish moments where I just want us to check out, sell everything and live

the rest of our days somewhere tropical - screw helping people, I want this man to MYSELF! But he would wither away without a battle to fight, so onward.

## CHAPTER SIX

# From Knowing Someone to Being Someone

The only way you move from Information to Transformation is via Revelation and Application.

—Dr. John A. King

Outside of a dog, a book is a man's best friend. Inside of a dog, it's too dark to read.

—Groucho Marx

In theory, there is no difference between theory and practice. In practice there is.

—Yogi Berra

I have always had walls full of books; I typically give away half of them every couple of years to make room for the new ones I need to buy and probably won't read for a year. One day I started doing my bi-annual clear out and began regrouping and reordering by books by topic. What I found challenged me. The area that I had targeted first to deal with was my self-esteem. I suffered incredibly from a problem with self-loathing and lack of self-worth. I had dozens of books on my shelves on this topic, books I had forgotten about, books I had studied and read - all containing information that never helped me deal with this issue.

Putting aside the recent events that gave me the why to the issue of low self-worth, I wanted to know, "Why was I never able to move beyond it?" I obviously recognized my low self-worth as something I needed to work on - I had dozens of books on the subject and spent hundreds of hours reading and researching about it. Where was my disconnect? I had the information but wasn't seeing the transformation.

Here is what I concluded: general INFORMATION has to become a personal REVELATION that must lead APPLICATION (or implementation), only then will the result be personal TRANSFORMATION.

Information: This is the process of gathering facts or of making facts known. Information is the building block and the starting point of all personal growth. You have to know who you are, where you want to go, and what it will look like when you get there. But to get there you have to identify what it is you don't even know that you need to know. You do this by increasing your knowledge base.

But information isn't enough. It is comparable to a guy sitting on the couch at night watching a Bowflex commercial and checking out his biceps. The guy thinks this information is good. He even knows this information is good. But it is still just information.

Revelation: This is information revealed as yours. It is an epiphany. It's the moment of truth. Revelation is when what you hear isn't just for everyone, it is just for you. You may have even heard it or read it before, but this time it is absolutely essential for YOU RIGHT NOW.

It is no longer just good information; it's your information. You now have understanding; you have insight.

There you are watching your Bowflex commercial again. This time the "Chariots of Fire Music" comes on, the lights dim, you put down the remote control, and you reach for the phone. Well, you try to reach for the phone, but you're too fat to make it. You scream, "Honey! I need a phone! A little help here! I am about to change my life."

You're going to do it. You know the Bowflex is for you. Or the butt master or whatever it is, you know it's for you. You got to have this. You got to do this. You need to change NOW!

Application: This is the moment of truth. You take the day off work and wait for UPS. The bell rings. The box is delivered. You now own the Bowflex Super Premium with Bonus Platinum Shaky Weight add-on.

You put it in the living room in front of the TV and there it sits as a footstool until it gets slid under the bed with the Fat Melter Belt 4000 (batteries not included).

Nothing changes. Why?

Because owning a Bowflex and using a Bowflex, are two different things.

Application: This is putting revelation to use. Only after INFORMATION becomes REVELATION, and then goes through the process of APPLICATION, does it lead to personal TRANSFORMATION. It's at this point, and only at this point, that you start to see your life change.

Transformation: This isn't something you make happen. It's not a thing you do. TRANSFORMATION is a by-product. It is the love child of the application of revealed information. I had shelves full of information; I even knew it was information I needed to have, so I had the revelation part, what I obviously never did though was apply it to my life.

So I developed a 21-day, 10-step program to instantly, 100% change my life overnight, for all time, without any effort.

## HOW TO REPROGRAM YOUR MIND

I lied. The 21-day, 10-step program to instantly 100% change your life overnight, for all time without any effort is total rubbish. I only said that because if the title were, "Things you have to do every day for the rest of your life," you'd probably throw yourself on the floor and start screaming for the "Instant Gratification Nanny."

So I didn't. Instead, I lied to you. All that crap about 21 days to break a habit, 21 days to make a habit, is just that, crap. If you believe in that rubbish, you will have 42 days of misery, followed by bitter disappointment in the first 24 hours after that. You might as well just start out by deciding you're going to take as much time as needed to change your life for the better, forever.

This section is a muddling of sorts or hodge-podge, which is defined as:

- A dialectical concept in Discordianism that posits that the tendency for restriction and control in society is matched proportionately by a counter-resulting tendency for chaos and randomness; and vice-versa.[48]

Or

- A muddled-together bunch of stuff.

The following is a collection of steps I took, or a developmental plan to give me a map for moving forward. I could try and fancy it up and impress you with an infographic, but I don't think it

---

48 Urban Dictionary. http://www.urbandictionary.com/define. php?term=hodge+podge

would add any value. I hope you're going to use this information, write all over the pages and make it better and applicable for yourself. When you do, please send it back to me, and I'll post it on my website.

Before you read any further, you have to promise yourself one thing: when you fail, or fall off the wagon so to speak, which you will, you are not allowed to be negative or self-condemning in any way. That won't help anyone. The only way you fail at this is by not trying. It's a journey, and you're going to make it. Today is a starting point, and by tomorrow you will be one step further down the road. If today doesn't go as planned, you will have a better idea on how to start tomorrow. People get so pissed off at me for some reason when I tell them to relax, don't be hard on themselves, and that it'll all work out in the end. It's like people want it to be hard or they want permission never to improve the quality of their lives, because they enjoy being a victim so much.

Relax, just try it, and trust it will work out. What have you got to lose, except being a pain in the arse to everyone else in your life?

## ME COACHING ME (PART 1): <u>The First 7 Actionable Steps</u>

My background is in corporate training and coaching. I developed this first set of 7 points like I was preparing a coaching session for myself. That's right; I was my own coach and my own client. I know, sounds a bit crazy, but hey, I have a mental illness - using the superpower BABY!

*And it went a bit like this:*

**Step 1: John, don't panic, you have a lot to re-learn, and it's going to take time and input from others.**

You have to surround yourself with people who speak into your life. But they must be the type of people who will talk to you about your weaknesses, while believing in your strengths. These people have to have a vested interest in your survival.

Not the survival of your corporate training business or your church or your status quo, but of you.

Qualities they need to have:

- They love you.
- They believe in you.
- They want to see you make it.
- They want your marriage to succeed.
- They want your dreams to stay alive.

You are going to have to trust them, and you don't trust anyone. I know it's a catch 22. So start by picking one person that you are pretty sure you can most probably, reasonably, nearly certainly, with a high degree of probability, TRUST - and actually trust them. Trust them to help you get past the paranoia and fear, to making a short list of people who will form your BRAINS TRUST. Why do you need a BRAINS TRUST? Because you, John, can't trust your brain at the moment.

I know, I know, what if they screw you over, well that won't be the first time you were screwed by someone you loved - get it? Joke? I made a crude reference to your abuse. Ok, not so funny, I thought it was, don't be such a pansy about it, I'm doing this for free.

**Step 2: You are going to have to change your perspective, on just about everything.**

You're not allowed to whine about your problems anymore. You can only celebrate change and victory. You can discuss the challenges you might experience in overcoming your issues, but not the failure you feel today if you struggle because you will have those days.

Don't allow yourself to be dissuaded or discouraged from a human standpoint. Start to see your life again with eternal ramifications, and that regardless of how dark it seems; you are journeying under a mightier light than that of your temporal conditions.

**Step 3: No longer call or see things as obstacles or disabilities; but as opportunities for growth.**

John, every person you ever admired overcame mountains, not molehills. Be that person for others. Suck it up and just get after it, mate. There are other men and women out there whose lives are screwed up, and you can help them.

Remember you're resilient, you're relentless, and you're tough. This thing hasn't beaten you so far; it's not bloody likely to now that you know what you are dealing with.

**Step 4: Make a plan and work the plan; include a RELATIONAL ASSET inventory.**

You have a habit of over-estimating what you can do in a year and under-estimating what God can do in 10 years.

When you hit a roadblock, make a detour. Use the situation you are in as a fulcrum to rise above it. You have to learn to tune out the negative voices in your life. In fact, you have to eliminate them and focus on what's real. Remember what Mona said, "... John, most of what you think is total bullshit - your head's a mess" - that's why you have a BRAINS TRUST.

Select the people who will make up your RELATIONAL ASSET inventory. Ask yourself, what relationships do you have that you can draw on? What untapped skills do you have? You have spent a lifetime helping people. It's time to cash in some chips and leverage them to help you win the fight.

The people in your RELATIONAL ASSET inventory are a level below your BRAINS TRUST, so do NOT spill your guts to them. Most folks won't cope. With these people, just talk to them about repositioning yourself and ask for their input and suggestions. Do NOT come across as needy. People don't like that. You're not needy; you just need their input and direction. People love it when you make them feel important. Never take money from them. Take advice and opportunity. The money you can get from somewhere else; input and opportunity are rare and precious gifts.

### Step 5: Vulnerability is not weakness; it is strength.

Whether it's your BRAINS TRUST or the RELATIONAL ASSET people, you're going to have to let people in. You are going to have to get comfortable sharing your whole story or part of it and even with confessing to weaknesses. It will be tough, and it will take courage. But the strongest people you have ever met have also been the most vulnerable. Just remember, do not, under any circumstance, do it to everyone, and never all in one sitting.

You scared the crap out of Mona; you'd scar some of these people for life.

**Step 6: You got to be able to measure it.**

When you work out, you go to the gym with your program already written out. You record the weights you lift, the sets you do, and over time you can track your progress. You are going to have to develop a way to measure your progress. (I used the "Life Wheel" below to establish a baseline and track development.)

If in four or eight weeks' time you can look back and see your progress, you will see how far you have come, and you can remind yourself of that on difficult days. The other thing is you're going to have to trust the people in your BRAINS TRUST when they tell you how far you have come.

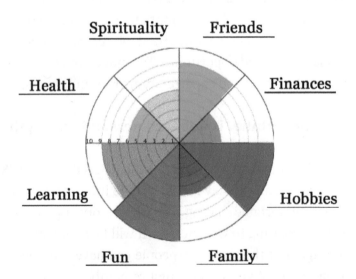

**Step 7: Start to dream again of your future.**

Thinking of the future is a tough one for you right now, but it's probably the most important item on your list so far.

You got to dream again, you have to. You are dying on the inside. You have always pushed yourself in the belief and hope that tomorrow was going to be better. When the shit hit the fan, all that stopped and you went into survival mode. I know you, and if you are not preparing for tomorrow, you'll end up dying one day at a time.Life is a fight, get back in the ring, tuck your chin and throw punches.

## ME COACHING ME (part 2): <u>The Mental Detox Program</u> <u>with 10 more Actionable Steps</u>

I came up with this plan after I realized the first one was a good general outline, but that I needed to be more specific, and according to my coaching session with myself, I had to make sure that what I did was measurable. As I mentioned before, I had a problem with how I spoke about myself, and my situation, so I decided to focus on that first. I asked myself, "How long would it take me to break a habit of negative self-talk?"

*Thus, I started my research into solving this question...*

Max Maltz was a cosmetic surgeon who wrote a self-help book [49]in the 1960's. He suggested that it takes 21 days to break a habit. (Maybe that is for pimple cream application, who knows?)

Timothy A. Pychyl suggested, "Six months minimum, and that's only if you're committed to the change and you are conscientious in your practice of a strategy for change."[50] (Okay, that is long, but doable.)

David DiSalvo said, "None of us ever truly 'breaks' a habit in the sense we mean by the term."[51] (Well that's depressing.)

---

49 Maltz, Maxwell, M.D., F.LC. S, "The New Psycho Cybernetics," 2001. Penguin Putnam, Inc.

50 Pychyl, Timothy. Quoted on http://www.hopesandfears.com/hopes/now/ question/216479-how-long-does-it-really-take-to-break-a-habit

51 DiSalvo, David. Quoted on http://www.hopesandfears.com/hopes/now/ question/216479-how-long-does-it-really-take-to-break-a-habit

I liked what I read by Toni Bernhard. It made sense to me and gave me hope: "How long it takes to break a habit depends on your willingness to make the effort. The key is to start small. Every time you make an effort to break a negative habit, you're laying down a new groove in your mind. Even a small groove makes it easier to break the negative habit the next time. As you do this over and over, the groove gets deeper and deeper until you've truly changed the way your mind reacts."[52]

I was willing, but I am a goal guy, and the thought of spending my life trying to make an ever-deepening groove with no end in sight wasn't going to work for me. Seeing as none of the experts could agree, and no one had a solid answer, I thought I'd do what they seem to do: MAKE IT UP AS I GO ALONG.

Maltz said it would take 21 days to BREAK a habit, some meme somewhere said it would take 14 days to MAKE a habit, so I settled on 35 days. At the end of these 35 days, I wasn't expecting to make/break a habit. I was just planning to have started to settle into my groove and to get myself going in a new direction in a single area of my life.

I needed a plan for when I screwed up. Because I told myself in Actionable Step 2 that I would. Some other guy somewhere said that if I made a mistake and slipped back into old habits, I would have to start back at the beginning. I thought that was pretty bogus and decided he could bite his bum and erased my browser history for the hour.

52 Bernhard, Toni, J.D. Quoted on http://www.hopesandfears.com/hopes/now/question/216479-how-long-does-it-really-take-to-break-a-habit

If I am preparing for a bodybuilding competition, and I am cutting weight and cave in and eat a brownie, that doesn't mean I have undone three weeks of weight loss. It just means I ate a brownie and have to get back on the wagon. It might cost me an extra hour of cardio tomorrow, but that's about it. It's different if I eat a brownie a day - THAT defeats the purpose.

When cutting weight, you often give yourself a cheat day once a week. So I decided to give myself three cheat days (or Homer Simpson "DOH!" days) during those 35 days of working out. That might seem dumb, because these disciplines aren't inter-related, but the experts didn't know what they were talking about, and I needed to make this work for me.

*Resulting Formula*: 21 days to break a habit + 14 days to make a habit + 3 'DOH!' days = 38 days to make it all priceless in the end.

The following is the **Mental Detox Program** I developed for myself with 10 more Actionable Steps. I programmed these Steps into every day when necessary or applicable. I scheduled them on my calendar before I did anything else. These simple Steps have become guidelines I still live by to this day. You'll also notice a rating alongside each Step. That's how well I think I'm doing in this area so far this year (2017).

**Step 1: Shut up!** 6/10

For the next 24 hours, you're not allowed to speak negatively about anything. Not the news, not the economy, not your health, your future, your family. If you want to have a rant about the state of the world and your life you can do it in your prayer time with God. He will probably tell you to shut up, too, because you've been

talking about the same crap for years. Why don't you try taking Him for coffee and telling Him a joke or something?

(I did this for a lot of years. I have some funny stories I'll tell you another time about the reactions of people when they saw me in my local cafe sitting alone at a table with 2 cups of coffee laughing hysterically at a joke everybody else seemed to think I was telling myself.)

**Step 2: Speak out!** 8/10

My Nanna used to say, "If you have nothing good to say, it is better to say nothing at all." But nature abhors a vacuum; it's not enough to stop something, I had to start something. I needed to speak positively every day about everything.

I would go out of my way to find something positive to say about people I met or situations I found myself in. I was amazed at how this brought almost instant results. I became more positive and found myself looking at life in a much more favorable manner.

**Step 3: Every day write in your journal and say one positive thing you believe you will be or do in your future.** 8/10

This isn't an exercise in egotism; it's an attempt to develop or establish a wholesome self-respect for my God-given gifts and talents.

I wrote this program sometime in 2011, and at that time, I decided to believe that somehow the horror of my past could be used to help myself and others have a positive future. The only positive thing I could come up with to say about what I was going through

was, "I believe that one day, all things will turn around for good." That was it, that's all I had. I would write it and say it every day.

During this time, I came to understand that success happens when preparedness meets opportunity. If I were not trying in some way to position myself for my future, I would never be ready to make the most of the possibilities when they present themselves. I didn't know what I was going to do in the years ahead. I knew that at that time, outside of the jobs I was working, I could write poetry. I could publish them anonymously on a website and a couple of social media accounts in an attempt to help people who'd gone through the sort of things I had; so every day I worked on that.

In November 2015, I got the email and the invitation to participate in the *Stopping Traffic* documentary. If I hadn't been writing, thinking, praying, believing, and doing social media talking about my journey, I would never have been in a position to make the most out of this opportunity. Friend, I sit here writing this in 2017, and I can tell you with absolute certainty: THAT SIMPLE PRAYER FROM A BROKEN MAN WAS THE VERY THING THAT OPENED THE DOOR TO A FUTURE, WHICH IS FAR GREATER THAN ANYTHING I COULD EVER HAVE HOPED FOR OR IMAGINED.

### Step 4: Feed the Inner Man. 9/10

As you would feed your body at least three times a day; you must feed your mind.

## First Meal - Bible before breakfast

I would make coffee, take my Bible and sit down somewhere calm and relaxing. I needed it to be as noise-free as possible. I would slowly read. If I read four chapters, great; if I read four verses and sat there just thinking about them, better. If you're not a Christian, then find something that speaks to your inner Self on a spiritual level.

## Second Meal - Get a good book

It didn't matter if it were a print copy for reading or an audio book that I'd listen to on the way to work. It just had to be something I was interested in, something positive and instructive. Topics I read then and still do today are about leadership, biographies, self-help — anything that would be useful in my future.

## Third meal - A butt-kicking fiction novel

It didn't matter if it were about an alien invasion or a Dean Koontz/Stephen King suspense book. Books, to me, are movies for the mind. I could watch a movie and still be thinking about other stuff. I could not be reading about psycho gypsies driving a possessed car with a zombie rabid St. Bernard in the passenger seat, while being chased by some kid that sees ghosts, and be thinking about anything else.

Don't under-estimate the importance of reading fiction. This time was just as important for reprogramming my mind as the other two *meals*. I normally read this before I went to sleep. It was light entertainment compared to my nightmares.

## Step 5: Run away. 7/10

I made up my mind that I would avoid arguments, contention, strife, and negativity whenever possible. If I found myself caught up in the middle of a negative exchange, I'd find a positive way to excuse myself from the conversation or situation, or simply get up and walk away. I didn't have to sit and listen to other people whine and bitch about others. I didn't have the bandwidth for it, and I just didn't need it. So I didn't buy into it.

## Step 6: Friends don't let other friends be losers all their lives. 9/10

Get a Let's No Longer Be Losers (LNLBL) partner or partners. I committed to being in contact with someone every day for the full 38 days. I would text or send an email every day, and at least once a week, we would get together and chat.

The focus of these communications was to tell my partner how yesterday went, what I was working on today, and what my goal was for tomorrow. I was trying to establish good, forward-thinking habits.

Why only 38 days? Because life moves quickly and I wanted an out in case things got uneasy or difficult. What I didn't need was a further level of stress if my LNLBL partner(s) didn't work out. On the other hand, if I could find someone to walk with me long-term until I was out of this hole, then that would be helpful. I was fortunate to find three people who after eight years are still walking with me.

## Step 7: Make a list – Nice and Naughty. 10/10

I made a *nice* list of friends and acquaintances, determined who were the most positive thinkers, and deliberately cultivated a relationship with them. I took them for coffee, bought lunch, and went to the movies. I tried not to talk too much about what I was currently facing. The aim at the time was to develop a network of future-looking, non-taxing, replenishing relationships.

I am not suggesting that I hid things or wasn't honest with them if asked how I was progressing. But I was aware that I was at the bottom of a hole, and it would be easy to talk or think only about that hole, which would be boring for them.

Look, regardless of what they say, most people don't give a crap, and when they ask you, "How are you doing?" They just want you to say, "Good," so they can tell you how awesome they are. So enjoy them for who they are: awesome, positive, fun-loving, movie-going, all-round good-timing friends.

With the *naughty* (negative) list of people, I didn't abandon them; I just learned to manage them. I discovered that all relationships tend to have one of three dynamics at any one time:

- You will always have people or relationships when *you* are taking from *them*. This could be a boss, friend, parent, maybe even a partner (for a period).
- Then there are others who offer a give-and-take relationship that's mutually satisfying and beneficial.
- Then there are those who *take* from *you*. You'll be drained after every interaction with them.

Some relationships will change over time and with maturity. I'm not suggesting you eliminate everyone out of your life who's not giving you something in one way or another. I believe a great blessing comes when we give something to someone who's unable to give something to us in return. What I am encouraging you to do is to deliberately build relationships with people who are going where you want to go and be aware of the amount of time you spend with *takers*.

## Step 8: Actively engage in the admiration of others. 10/10

Let great men and women shape your life and point you towards a possible future. Never be too big a woman/man to allow yourself to be inspired by the life struggles and victories of others. During this period, I read biographies of great leaders who overcame tough circumstances. Their successes encouraged me and gave me hope.

I'm not suggesting you should be awestruck by other people and try to copy them. Remember that most people, despite their confident appearance and demeanor, are often just as scared as you are and just as doubtful of themselves. What I am suggesting however, is that it's okay to look at the lives of those you admire and mimic the attitudes of those who continuously produce success or overcome adversity. We can cut our learning curve by up to 90% by studying their mistakes and by letting their successes encourage us.

## Step 9: Actively cancel out any bad or negative thought. 6/10

This one was hard for me: Formulate and stamp indelibly on your mind a mental picture of yourself as succeeding. Hold this picture tenaciously. Never permit it to fade. If you do this, then your mind will seek to develop this picture. Never think of yourself failing - never doubt the reality of the mental image. Doubting is dangerous; your mind will always try to complete what it pictures. So always picture SUCCESS, no matter how bad things seem to be going at the moment.

My LNLBL partners had to help me with this one because my mind was trained for so long to focus on failure.

## Step 10: Pray positive prayers. 7/10

I also had to change the way I prayed, reminding myself that God was with me. The easiest way to do this was to let my prayers take the form of thanksgiving based on the assumption that God wants to, and is, in the process of giving me (and you) great and wonderful things.[53]

What to do if you muck it up?

Well, you have 3 "DOH!" Days (you'll need about 4 million).

If you muck it up (and you will), if you fall back into a negative space or mindset (and you will) - relax, get up, and go again. It is that simple. The only thing you can expect with 100% certainty

---

53 Matthew 9:29; Romans 8:31

is that you will make a mistake, and that you won't get it right, so be prepared to cut yourself some slack. We all fail at different times, but you are trying, and just by trying you are succeeding.

One of the hardest challenges I had during my early stages of recovery was living under a cloud of externally imposed perfection. I knew I wasn't perfect; I knew there were difficulties. I knew it was a challenge to live with me. I couldn't change that, I wanted to, but I couldn't. It seemed like nothing I did was ever good enough. Affection was withdrawn, support was withdrawn, and encouragement was withdrawn.

I realized and came to accept two things:

- I was spending all my time looking for external validation and affirmation; and
- I was not benchmarking or celebrating my successes and progress internally.

The day I stopped these two things was the day I decided that every time I failed, I would fail forward. I became comfortable with failure when it got me closer to my goals. Some days I would walk forward, some days crawl, and some days I dragged myself along the ground. But I didn't care as long as I was doing my best to move forward.

When I decided that my validation and celebration of progress needed to come from me (not externally), it immediately took the performance pressure away. I was able to celebrate even the smallest victory, like going to the grocery store for sausages on my own, with near hilarious joy. Nine years later, this is still the

case. Each day I am thankful for many things. There are many things that I am doing today that I never thought I would do again, and there are so many things that I have seen come back to me in greater abundance.

## MEL'S TURN

We are accustomed to getting things fast. We microwave our food, we order our Starbucks drink online because we can't stand queues, and we expect our Amazon Prime order to qualify for same-day delivery. The thought of working a 10-step anything, taking every thought captive, watching what we say, and taking input from others on the whole process can seem exhausting. Isn't there some shortcut?

Nope. Re-programming your mind takes time and hard work. John has spent years, literally thousands of hours, helping me with how I think about myself - particularly about my body. He had been slogging away with me for so long; I think he was almost bewildered when the effort finally paid off. The percolation was internal; I had started to be kinder to myself in my thoughts, but he didn't see anything happening. Then, bam, I turned 40. I decided, "I'm too old to think poorly about myself anymore. I'm done with that crap." And so I was.

My lifelong struggle with food, starvation, and self-loathing was over. I was about a 7- or 8-year overnight success. If I can change, so can you. The process works. Commit to the effort. What do you have to lose?

## CHAPTER SEVEN

# Happiness, Unicorns and Other Myths

For what does it profit a man to gain the whole world and forfeit his soul?

—Jesus of Nazareth

The secret to happiness is freedom...and the secret to freedom is courage.

—Thucydides

Success is getting what you want. Happiness is wanting what you get.

—Dale Carnegie

## WHAT IS HAPPINESS?

"Life, liberty and the pursuit of happiness," would have to be one of the best-known phrases in modern history. It stands for opportunity and possibility. It has come to mean so much more than the American Dream; it is the dream and hope for all free people around the world. This phrase gives us examples of what the American founding fathers called "unalienable rights;" that is what they believed were the natural and legal rights given to us as human beings by God that should be protected by the government.

Life, I understand; Liberty, I appreciate; Happiness, seemed like a fleeting dream. It was the shallow quest at the bottom of a bottle, or what I looked for after two hours at the gym but didn't get. It was a hole that sex didn't fill or money couldn't buy. Maybe I was born that way, maybe it was because of the circumstances of my childhood. But now I was unhappy with being unhappy - I think the clinical term is fucking miserable - and I didn't want to be that any more.

Others would talk about how I could never change and how it was probably best if I just accepted this and got some medication to *level me out*. When people described me they would say that my personality was somewhat melancholy. I know I sometimes gave in to periods of introspection and dark moods. I don't think I qualified as being clinically depressed; I was just morbidly unhappy, which was expected of me and for me for the rest of my life.

Herein was the challenge: I didn't know what it meant to be happy. I didn't have a before picture to compare my *now* to; therefore, I didn't have an idea of what the future could look like. For all

their advice, the normal people around me didn't seem to be any better off. Most of them didn't come across as happy. They constantly talked about there never being enough time as they were too busy working because there was never enough money.

In 2017, there will likely be twice as many suicides as homicides in the U.S.[54] In 2008, our doctors wrote 164 million prescriptions for anti-depressants.[55] We have more money, education, science, and opportunities than ever in our history; and yet, we are a nation that is increasingly dissatisfied. Happiness is not increasing in our society, but depression and anxiety are.

The World Health Organization predicts that by 2020, depression will be the second-largest cause of disability. In 2010, a survey said that 60% of American students graduating felt hopeless. According to a Marist-McClatchy Poll[56] conducted in 2014, 78% of Americans think it's harder now than in previous generations to get ahead. In a 2013 Harris Poll, only 30% of Americans said they were happy.[57]

---

54 Centers for Disease Control, https://www.cdc.gov/nchs/fastats/homicide.htm; https://www.cdc.gov/nchs/fastats/suicide.htm

55 "Consumer Reports: Antipsychotic drug has risks, high price," Washington Post, November 24, 2009. http://www.washingtonpost.com/wp-dyn/content/article/2009/11/20/AR2009112003514.html

56 Lightman, David. "McClatchy-Marist Poll: American dream seen as out of reach," February 13, 2014. http://www.mcclatchydc.com/news/nation-world/national/economy/article24763519.html

57 Gregoire, Carolyn. "Happiness Index: Only 1 In 3 Americans Are Very Happy, According To Harris Poll," June 1, 2013. http://www.huffingtonpost.com/2013/06/01/happiness-index-only-1-in_n_3354524.html

So if the *normal* people weren't happy, and I wasn't happy, maybe people across the board were struggling with what happiness was and how to be happy? Was happiness just a bedtime story you told your kids? Was real happiness something that we as a society had lost along the way?

## Defining Happiness.

There are nearly 175,000 titles on Amazon that include the word happy; be it a Guide to, the Art of, Steps to, or Secrets of, happiness. I bought a dozen of the best reviewed and best rated, including the ones for idiots, morons and fools - all of which are guaranteed to bring me happiness. There seemed to be a consensus across these tomes of self-improvement that a person's happiness was made up of what I called the Big Three:

- Money
- Image
- Status or Popularity

Apparently, if anyone had these three things, then they would be happy. I thought that was bogus. I had money, not as much as some, but certainly more than others. In my circle, I had image, reputation, and status and popularity; yet, I couldn't ever remember being truly content.

So I started to look elsewhere, and I found some fascinating and challenging material.

## Rating Happiness.

My first find was something called the Happy Planet Index (HPI).[58]
The HPI collected information from across the globe from various
sources and rated happiness according to several factors. Those
factors included the well-being of its citizens (Gallup World
Poll); the life expectancy of its citizens (United Nations Survey);
a nation's impact on its environment (Global Footprint Network);
and something called Inequality of Outcomes which looks at the
different classes of people within a country and compares them with
each other. It combines all of these factors and rates participating
countries around the world. I did my original research in 2013,
and the figures below are from the latest report, 2016.

According to the HPI, the happiest nation in the world is Costa
Rica with a score of 44.7. Compare this to the lowest, Chad, with a
Happiness Index of only 1.5. What surprised me were the ratings
of some of the other countries, including our own. For example:

- Switzerland: 34.3
- Australia: 21.2
- USA: 20.7
- Afghanistan: 20.2
- Rwanda: 19.5

Yes, you did read that correctly, the USA is only 0.5 points ahead
of Afghanistan on the Happy Planet Index, and we are only 1.2
points ahead of Rwanda. I found this very hard to believe. I
couldn't imagine we were that close to nations that had experienced
genocide or in the midst of civil war for decades. So I did what

---

58 http://happyplanetindex.org

every researcher does, I went looking for data to support the conclusion I wanted. I found the Happiness Report and things didn't get any better.

The Happiness Report (HR)[59] is part of a global initiative for the United Nations. It assigns countries a Happiness Rank based on a nation's sense of caring, personal freedom, generosity, honesty, health, income, and good governance. It surveys a total of 155 countries. I started back with the initial reports of 2007, and I liked what I found, the Good Old USA was sitting in 3rd place.

Americans can tolerate a bronze medal every now and again, but we are a nation of winners, and I knew that things had to get better. We could probably look back in history and blame George W. Bush for our bad rating. We knew everything else was his fault; but then we had Obama, and he promised to change everything. We weren't sure what changed, exactly, but it was definitely "Change we could believe in."

The 2016 report came out, and America didn't do so well. We now ranked #14 in the world, but that wasn't the fascinating thing for me. What I found fascinating were the countries whose overall happiness had increased, while ours had decreased. Places like Guatemala, Uruguay, and Afghanistan had increased in happiness. The one that blew me away was Syria. Syria in the midst of a civil war had seen a 4-point increase[60] in its overall rating since 2007.

The Big Three things I was told would make up and guarantee my happiness, I just couldn't see being the factor that led to the

---

59 http://worldhappiness.report
60 https://en.wikipedia.org/wiki/World_Happiness_Report

change in ratings of these countries. My conclusion was that if I were finding it so hard to quantify what made people happy in America, maybe I was starting in the wrong place? Maybe I should start with what makes people unhappy?

## What is making us unhappy?

Researching what made us so unhappy proved to be a fascinating and very eye-opening experience for me. What I found were five principles that gave insight into what being unhappy actually was.

## Principle 1: We live from the outside-in.

Sound familiar? It's that whole tapestry thing again.

According to a 2014 study in the journal Social Forces[61], just 6% of adults end up doing something they like with their lives. If you read across a range of different publications, there are all sorts of reasons. The prevailing one is that by the nature of our society we look for the answers to happiness as being external to ourselves. That is why people believe if they had a new car or a bigger house or a different job they wouldn't be depressed or miserable. The reality is that once we obtain these so-called answers, they rarely if ever, affect our emotional state significantly or positively. In fact, most people who live from the outside-in often get more depressed because the things they thought would make a difference in how they feel about life and their future end up having no real impact on them at all. I think Jim Carey put it very well when he said: "I think everybody should get rich and

61 https://academic.oup.com/sf

famous and do everything they ever dreamed of so they can see that it's not the answer."

## Principle 2. We are unhappy because we are told that life isn't messy.

Disappointment arises out of unmet expectations.

Somewhere along the way, someone painted a picture for us that life was going to be easy. All we had to do was climb on the post-graduate highway (high school or college), hit cruise control, and we'd get to where we were supposed to go without any major calamities. We may choose to take the side ramp to marriage, or stop at a strip mall and pick up a couple of kids, but basically, we were taught that if we study hard, clean our teeth and were "nice" people, we would safely arrive at retirement happy and satisfied. We all know this is just not the case. We all know now that life has more twists and turns than it does straight ways, and we were never prepared for them.

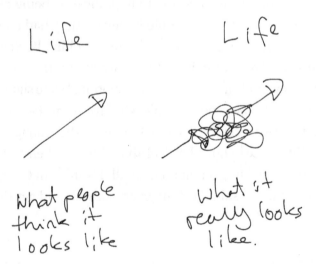

## Principle 3: We are unhappy because we have too many choices.

Remember the day when all you did on a telephone was make a call? When you could go to the bathroom, and no one could locate you? Remember how there were only 10 different cookies at your corner store? Now we have 350 varieties of cookies, 40 different kinds of toothpaste, 120 different salad dressings, and 159 different soda or drink options.

Since the time of Adam and Eve, we have convinced ourselves that maximizing our happiness is connected with having a multitude of choices. The greater the number of choices; the better off we think we'll be. We don't ever question this; in fact, we see this as the cornerstone of our material western culture and life. Barry Schwartz calls this phenomenon the "dogma of the western world."[62]

Having too many choices causes three conjunctive challenges in a person's life, which I reframe as:

*Emotional Paralysis* (EP)

Believe it or not, with so many options to choose from, it makes it harder, not easier, to decide what you like or what might make you happy. I'm sure you've experienced this?

*Fear Of Missing Out* (FOMO)

FOMO prohibits satisfaction as people report being less satisfied with the choices they ultimately make because they are always

---

62 https://www.ted.com/talks/barry_schwartz_on_the_paradox_of_choice

wondering if the second choice or the third choice would have been better and would have made them happier. This FOMO induces a weird sort of buyers-regret cycle where someone is continually second-guessing what was probably a good decision. The cycle robs them of the satisfaction that should come with the choice they made.

*Perfection Becomes Expectation* (PBE)

With all of the options we now have available, our expectations become escalated. We are no longer satisfied with a pair of jeans, a nice cell phone, or a welcoming home. We have to search for the perfect jeans, the perfect phone, and the perfect house. When perfection becomes the expectation, individuals end up hoping that they're not too badly disappointed with what they end up choosing. Yet, when there was only one hamburger joint, one pair of jeans, or one cell phone to buy and that item didn't live up to your expectations because of its poor performance and/or quality, it was the service provider's fault. Now, when the whatever-it-is doesn't live up to your expectations, we internalize and make it our fault because we should have taken the second or third option.

Subsequently, I found that EP, FOMA, and PBE challenges are not a worldwide issue; but rather spectacular examples of a first-world problem, peculiar to industrial societies with material affluence. In countries not as prosperous as America, where just having enough food for one meal a day is a blessing, people tend to be thankful for what little they have. Some clinical psychologists believe that these three challenges impact so greatly in some people that they lead to clinical depression and suicide. When you stop and think about what the HPI and the HR were indicating, it all starts to make sense.

## Principle 4: We are unhappy due to nature or nurture

*Nature* is what we have at birth: our genes, our personality, our dispositions towards certain things; later you will see this referred to as a GENETIC SET POINT. *Nurture* is how we develop as a person based on our family environment and the things we are exposed to as children. Both, nature and nurture, play an important role in how we interact with the world and how the world interacts with us.

The filter or the gate that often dictates our response in a given situation is our emotions. Our emotions are, by and large, the result of either nature or nurture. A human being is capable of experiencing both positive and negative emotions. These emotions make up a total system and this system is far more than what we reduced them to when we call them *feelings*.

Let's use the *Fight or Flight Response* example from earlier on. Fight or Flight (or hyper arousal) is a physiological reaction that occurs in response to a perceived harmful event, attack, or threat to survival. It is a system of alerts based on memory and experience, and it flavors how we perceive things and the decisions we make.

You can be unhappy because you are in a state of constant fear or paranoia because it's part of your *nature* - the personality you were born with - or you could be like that because it's a result of your *nurture*. The good news is that when either of these negatively affects you, both can be remedied. You can, in fact, learn to manage your responses. We will talk about that in a bit.

## Principle 5: We are unhappy because we don't understand unhappiness.

In 1998, Martin Seligman was appointed the president of the American Psychological Association. He chose as the theme for his term something called Positive Psychology. Positive Psychology is concerned with what holds the greatest value to us in life, or the factors that contribute the most to a well-lived, fulfilling life. Seligman's colleague, Christopher Peterson, defines Positive Psychology as "the scientific study of what makes life most worth living."[63]

Seligman and Peterson realized that for the last 300 years, physiologists and scientists had just focused on the negative conditions that afflicted people. They concluded that people in their profession saw happiness and unhappiness as opposing endpoints on the same continuum.

They realized that this was wrong, and a person didn't instantly become happy the moment they stopped being miserable. A person who had been unhappy for an extended period of time accumulated learned behavioral responses, and they needed help to change. To help a patient re-engineer themselves mentally and emotionally, a doctor should spend as much time, if not more, helping him or her to recognize, to focus on, and to build the best aspects of themselves while simultaneously working on repairing the worst.

---

63 https://www.psychologytoday.com/blog/the-good-life/200805/what-is-positive-psychology-and-what-is-it-not

Think about it. It is logical. If you have been fearful your whole life because of something, taking that something away doesn't automatically give you the ability not to be scared, because scared is all you have ever known. What you end up doing is finding new things to be afraid of. Why? Because you take comfort in the known. You know how to act when you are scared. You know how it feels to be afraid.

This idea was a significant revelation for me. I realized that even when I was trying to be positive, I was focused on the negative feelings. I was doing things, eating things, wearing things, thinking things because I wanted to be less miserable; not so that I could be happy. When I came to understand that being *unhappy* was a habit I needed to break AND being *happy* was a skill I needed to learn, I felt an incredible sense of relief. I knew I wasn't happy, but now I understood I hadn't taught myself how to be happy; I had not yet acquired those skills.

## GETTING TO HAPPY

We all live with the objective of being happy; our lives are all different and yet the same.

—Anne Frank

I am more and more convinced that our happiness or unhappiness depends far more on the way we meet the events of life than on the nature of those events themselves.

—Wilhelm von Humboldt

We hold these truths to be self-evident that all men are created equal; that they are endowed by their Creator with certain inalienable rights; that among these are life, liberty, and the pursuit of happiness.

—U.S. Declaration of Independence

I love how the founding fathers put it; we have the right to pursue happiness, we don't have the right to have it.

**Pursuit**: The action of following or pursuing someone or something.

I felt that everything I had learned, studied, or tried had led me to this point. I now knew that I could make it, that I could turn my life around. I was going to be so much more than just a survivor. If I could just take my information that had become REVELATION and apply it, TRANSFORMATION would be the natural outcome.

I would spend the next six months reading, researching and writing, compiling ideas and strategies to get me from where I was to where I needed to be. Here are the 5 critical thoughts

and methodology I developed and implemented along the way that began with my question: "What makes up this thing called Happiness?"

**THOUGHT 1:**

Any discussion or research that I did on happiness always ended up mentioning dopamine. Dopamine is a chemical in the brain that is necessary for feelings of pleasure and happiness. Apparently, as we age, our ability to produce dopamine diminishes. If it diminishes too much, you end up with Parkinson's disease. The body adapts to what it needs and uses. If you are not doing things that produce dopamine, then your body says, "I don't need to keep producing this chemical." I call it the *use it or lose it* aspect of brain health and happiness.

Another thing I continued to find in my reading was something called being *in the zone*. People in sales books would talk about it, as would musicians, athletes, and writers; so it wasn't particular to an activity. Rather, it was particular to an attitude or a mental commitment. When you're *in the zone*, you're focused on and absorbed by, what you are involved in. You're fully engaged and time seems to stand still.

Apparently, this state of mind is reported to produce a sense of elation and fulfillment by releasing dopamine and bringing peace, clarity, and centeredness. When people are *in the zone*, they report feeling in control and forgetting their problems. In a sense, they forget themselves and become fully present in that moment. Having a hobby or activity that was consuming, something I could focus on or be passionate about was important; this made sense for me.

These are the activities I did on and off to keep me energized:

- Take up a new sport. I took up mountain biking, started to learn golf, and Mel wanted to try tennis, so I did that too.
- I changed my gym program every 6 weeks.
- I made a point of celebrating any work success because goal completion also increased dopamine production.
- I started to draw. I would start by copying other artists' line work, which was absorbing. I'm no forger, but Mel liked some enough that she has in her office.
- If I'm riding my bike or working out, I make sure to listen to music with a driving beat to get me going. Engaging music increases dopamine production as well.
- Mel and I try a new thing at least once a month. We might go with friends to a strange hole-in-the-wall cafe, see some obscure artist at the gallery, or visit a little playhouse.

These activities not only made life more diverse, but also got me out of my head and stimulated my body's natural dopamine production.

**THOUGHT 2:**

Tim Kasser is a professor of Psychology at Knox College in Galesburg, Illinois, specializing in materialism and well-being. In his study on *Happiness in America* he talked about two different kinds of goals or values that people have; he called these extrinsic and intrinsic goals or values.[64]

Intrinsic goals are the exact opposite of extrinsic goals. Extrinsic goals are things that are external to you. These are goals that

---

64 Kasser, Tim. *The High Price of Materialism,* 2003. The MIT Press.

are focused on rewards, material possessions or from which you gain external praise. Intrinsic goals are things that are satisfying in and of themselves, because they have to do with our internal physiological needs.

Remember those three things all the happiness books tell us we need? Those are extrinsic goals:

- Money
- Image
- Status or popularity

Here are examples of common intrinsic goals:

- Personal Growth - trying to be who I really am
- Mutually Beneficial Relationships - close and connected relationships that benefit all involved
- Community Feeling - a desire to help the world be a better place.

Research seems to indicate that the vast majority of people who are driven by extrinsic goals report less and less satisfaction with their lives. They tend to be more depressed, more anxious, and feel less vital or energized in life. (Put that in your pipe, happiness-book-writing-people.)

Those driven by intrinsic goals report feeling more vitality, a greater sense of general satisfaction, and are mostly happier than their extrinsic-goal-oriented counterparts. There doesn't appear to be a set formula for happiness, but there do seem to be a group of factors that are reported to make up standard building blocks of a happy life. (Anyone needing a hug right about now?)

These factors not only make us happy but they are free:

- Playfulness
- Having new experiences
- Friends and family
- Doing things that are meaningful
- Appreciating what we have
- Helping others succeed

## THOUGHT 3:

Martin Seligman describes happiness as having three parts: pleasure, engagement, and meaning.[65]

*Pleasure* is the feel good part of happiness. *Engagement* refers to living a good life of work, family, friends, and hobbies (total absorption in what we do). *Meaning* refers to using our strengths to contribute to a larger purpose.

## THOUGHT 4:

Richard Davidson, professor of Psychology and Psychiatry at the University of Wisconsin–Madison, suggests there is no difference between learning happiness and learning to play golf or a musical instrument. It is a skill that can be taught and learned.[66]

## THOUGHT 5:

Nancy Etcoff, assistant clinical professor of Psychology in the Department of Psychiatry at Harvard, notes that 50% of our

65 http://www.pursuit-of-happiness.org/history-of-happiness/martin-seligman-psychology/

66 "Professor Richard J. Davidson: 'Happiness Is A Skill That Can Be Learned,'" Huffington Post, January 24, 2014. https://www.huffingtonpost.com/2014/01/23/richard-j-davidson-davos_n_4636683.html

happiness appears to be genetic and personality-based. In other words, we are born with a certain disposition, and this aspect of ourselves is relatively difficult to change. However, of our total overall happiness, 40% comes from our activities and relationships and the final 10% from things like income and environment, which she calls circumstances (see Figure 3). What this meant to me: there was considerable scope and opportunity to increase my level of happiness through focus and hard work.

*Figure 3.* Happiness as per Etcoff

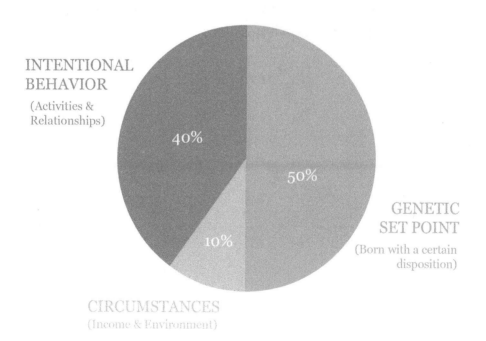

## MY CONCLUSIONS: THE HAPPINESS MODEL

For me, Nancy Etcoff's work was my tipping point. It gave me numbers and a breakdown of what makes up happiness. It was no longer an ethereal concept, but something that could be graphed and quantified. I needed to find a way to get my head around what all this research meant. I needed a way to simplify it all, so I developed a model with three straightforward formulas that dealt with different Happiness levels in my life: my overall happiness; my personal happiness; and my enduring sense of happiness.

When I drew The Happiness Model (see Figure 4), it reminded me of a triangular pyramid with the base being *happiness*, and each side of the triangle representing the different levels that made up my happiness in life.

# THE HAPPINESS MODEL

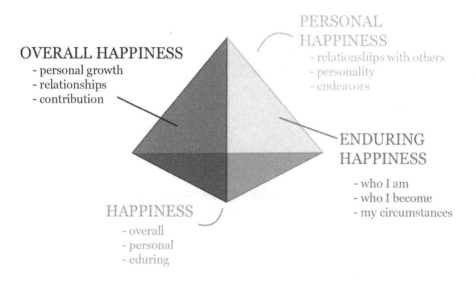

**OVERALL HAPPINESS**
- personal growth
- relationships
- contribution

PERSONAL
HAPPINESS
- relationships with others
- personality
- endeavors

ENDURING
HAPPINESS

- who I am
- who I become
- my circumstances

HAPPINESS
- overall
- personal
- eduring

*Figure 4.* The Happiness Model

## OVERALL HAPPINESS = PG+R+C

Overall Happiness is made up of three key elements (see Figure 5):

- <u>Personal Growth</u> - Working with what I've got. I had to be the best me I could be. I had to discover who I was and what I liked, and then be faithful to it.
- <u>Relationships</u> - I needed to make new, authentic, personal relationships, and where possible, by God's good grace and hard work, repair family relationships.
- <u>Contribution</u> – In order to make a contribution to others, I couldn't be so focused and consumed with my issues, even as overwhelming as they were and sometimes, still are. I needed to find a way, although it might only be small to start with, to make the world a better place.

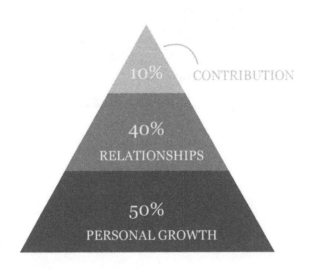

*Figure 5.* Overall Happiness

## PERSONAL HAPPINESS = O+P+E

Personal Happiness is made up of three elements (see Figure 6):

- <u>Others</u> - My interaction and relationship with others, whether they are family, friends, or work colleagues, reflects my contribution to the world. I feel compelled to help others and contribute to other people's success and fulfillment.
- <u>Personality</u> - My personality makes a significant contribution to my Personal Happiness. I know that nature and nurture predispose me to certain levels of Personal Happiness, which I need to learn to manage more effectively.
- <u>Endeavors</u> - My work, my job, my status in the community, and material possessions I have or need to have.

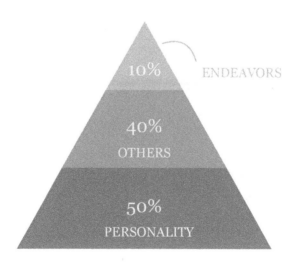

*Figure 6.* Personal Happiness

## ENDURING HAPPINESS=A+B+C

I realized that by this stage in my recovery, I was experiencing fleeting happiness, but I wanted something more. I wanted to replace the abiding sense of melancholy I experienced with what I termed Enduring Happiness. Enduring Happiness also consists of three key elements (see Figure 7):

- <u>Am</u> – This is who I am based on my DNA; how I was genetically born. It includes things like my intellect, personality, and predisposition to certain behaviors.
- <u>Become</u> – This is who I choose to become with the skills I can learn, activities I can engage in, and passions I can develop.
- <u>Circumstances</u> – These can't always be controlled, but I can control my responses to them.

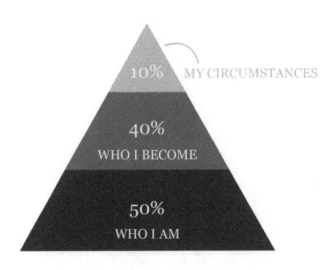

*Figure 7.* Enduring Happiness

When I started to think of the ramifications of these Happiness Levels and subsequent formulas (see Figures 5, 6 and 7), it struck me that these were principles that could help anyone who needed to overcome anything.

## Example 1: The Troubled Childhood

Let's say a child has a genetic set point of 20% happy. Her life pretty much sucks and is unchangeable for her; but (this is where it got exciting for me) if this child intentionally engaged in activities that increased dopamine; searched for and found something to be passionate about that would get her in the zone; and gave herself the learning skills she needed to be fulfilled; she could gain a full 40% extra of Enduring Happiness.

AND, if she worked hard and skillfully, set realistic material and social goals, she would have the potential to gain another 10% of Enduring Happiness.

That means this kid with an entirely sucky start in life could hit a whopping 70% of Enduring Happiness. Considering that 60% of the U.S. is unhappy, this *little loser* could rise from the bottom of the pile to the top of the heap with the other 30% of Americans who say they're happy.

## Example 2: Eeyore

Eeyore has 0% happy genes. Not only does his life suck, but he also sucks. But if he got focused on changing his outlook and activities in life, then Eeyore could increase his Enduring Happiness rating to 50%!

Now I know there are people out there who will say that no one can hit the maximum amount in any of the above areas, and you're probably right. But here is my response to you: "Piss off; I'm not interested."

The thought of even the slight possibility of being able to rebuild my life so that one day I might be 50% happy was all the motivation I needed.

### The realities of recovery

Let's hit pause for a minute, go grab a coffee, and let's have a chat - no seriously - make it a Bourbon if you need to.

Let's talk about the realities of recovery. If you have gotten this far in the book, you must like it or it was court-mandated. Either way, you probably have this sense that everything just keeps going around and around in circles. There is the occasional funny story, and there seems to be a little bit of movement. Then you read all the re-thinking programs and the happiness programs and you probably are hoping, "Here it comes - here is the part where it all comes together and he makes it over the hump!"

Let's put it in perspective. I was abused from ages 4-16. I lived as best I could on this foundation and the day-to-day impact it had on my personality and outlook on life from 16-45. Then John-A-Geddon happened from 45-48. Let's say for arguments' sake, I have been purposefully pursuing methods and insights for recovery from 49-54 (the age I am now). That's 6 years. So statistically, I have spent 11.1% of my life trying to figure this out.

I find that when I look back on my journey, it sometimes seems like 3 steps forward, 12 backward, fall on my face, crawl forward, and lie there exhausted for a week or 3. It really is that way, I suppose.

During those six years, I have gone around and around; up and down; tried, failed, tried, failed, failed, failed, and tried; over and over again. Friend, **THAT IS THE KEY TO FORWARD MOVEMENT**. Sheer bloody-mindedness. I still struggle, battle, run, claw, jump and fly forward, depending on the day.

Mel and I were sitting with Alicia and Ron the other night for dinner. They are the couple that make up my Back Deck Crew (BDC). They came over to talk about the book and how I could tweak it and polish it up.

Alicia is the engineer who says all the smart stuff, and she's the guardian of "The Spoon" (more on that later). Part way through dinner, she said, "John you are 80% better than you were when you first sat with us on the back deck 7 or 8 years ago." (Mel agrees and says I am a totally different person than the one she first met 9 years ago.)

Does it seem like I am going in circles with little progress? Yes, but that is the reality of life. I'm sorry, but it is just like that for me. Maybe it is for you as well — take courage and comfort that you are not alone.

## MEL'S TURN

John's natural set point is *not happy*. I'm a bit of a ying to his yang in this area – happy is my natural set point. He and his son call me "Little Miss Sunshine" because I wake up happy every day. But I can tell you, John's approach to happiness is just as focused and driven as any other goal he sets for himself. And the formula is the same: information, revelation, application, transformation. He will tell you that on most days he is 95-97% happy. What he's working on at this stage is not focusing too much on the 3-5%.

When John is having a tough day, I find it's helpful to tell him something I'm thankful for. Particularly something that has to do with him. I'll say something like, "I'm so thankful we can take 15 minutes together at the end of our day to swim in the pool. Thank you, Husband." It doesn't matter that the kids ran amuck, or the car mechanic called with bad news, or we STILL haven't changed the air filters in the A/C. We have those 15 minutes to be present together. Pointing out that I'm thankful for that time is something that I can do to help him meet his goals. Gently reminding him to be thankful lifts his eyes from the 5% bad, to the 95% good.

Another thing that we've committed to do, based on the research John has done, is limit our choices and simplify. We just don't let ourselves buy into FOMO (fear of missing out). We don't have cable TV - we stream everything so we can be intentional in what we watch (mostly documentaries). We ask ourselves before we buy something if we will still use it when we sell the house and move into an Airstream - this works for me. We both love old cars, so we don't buy new ones. We make fresh food from scratch because it's healthier and we don't have to stand in front of a

freezer or a row with hundreds of boxes in the grocery store and try to choose. And on, and on. Simpler is better.

Happiness and thankfulness are learned behaviors. Like any other thing you're trying to learn, like a foreign language, for example, it takes practice. And it helps to have someone to practice with.

## CHAPTER EIGHT

# This is Going to Hurt

Truth is everybody is going to hurt you: you just gotta find the ones worth suffering for.

—Bob Marley

Holding on to anger, resentment and hurt only gives you tense muscles, a headache and a sore jaw from clenching your teeth. Forgiveness gives you back the laughter and the lightness in your life.

—Joan Lunden

Chronologically, it was about two years after the recall event when I came to the understanding that I was going to deal with three recurring areas in my life:

- Trusting others;
- Forgiveness of others; and
- Bitterness/resentment toward others, i.e. an overwhelming sense of pissedoffedness.

The reality is, as I mentioned at the end of the last chapter, I still deal with issues like this regularly. They don't present the hourly problems they once did; it might only be once a day or once a week or month now. But I am aware that these three devils blunder around trying to get a foothold on every possible occasion.

Out of the three, I feel that forgiveness and bitterness are pretty much under control. I don't allow my mind or heart to dwell on past incidents that feed them. When they present themselves, it is more like a momentary flash that I have trained myself to dismiss in an almost off-handed way with phrases like, "I've dealt with that" or "I've moved on" or "I've forgiven myself."

If I am in an environment where I can say those affirmations out loud, I will. Rabbi Noah Weinberg put it this way, "Articulate your beliefs out loud. It bridges the gap between lofty notions of the soul and the world of reality. In other words, you'll find out if you really believe what you say."[67]

## The issue of trust

I think anyone who has been through anything similar to what I have experienced is expected to have trust issues. When you combine those with the impact of PTSD magnifying paranoia and fear, it makes trusting others a daily decision, not a natural inclination. That is what trusting others is to me, decisional.

---

67 http://www.aish.com/sp/48w/48970581.html

When I first experienced the recall, it impeded my ability to work, especially with others. I remember one occasion when I was speaking at church. At the end of the sermon, I stepped to one side of the pulpit and collapsed. The stress of standing in front of people, the pressure to make sure that what I was saying and doing was correct, and the cognitive effort to overcome my tendency to stutter, all proved to be too much, and my system overloaded. When that happened, I knew I needed to talk to my leadership team. It was time to "open the curtain" and tell them what I was dealing with on a daily basis. I thought that because we had been working together for several years, I could trust them. I very quickly learned that was not the case.

As a result of my confiding in them, I had team members say, "I didn't sign on for this," and leave. There were others who somehow felt God was telling them to start a church and take as many people with them as they could. The conversations they had went like this: "I can't really tell you what is going on, but Pastor John is sick, and we think it is God's plan for us to move on, and we *feel* you are supposed to come with us." Bloody cowards.

As a result, the church split and my stress increased. I got sicker, my then-wife at the time was heartbroken, and my kids were shattered. It was two more years before I took a chance on trusting someone again, and five or six more years before my kids were back in church. It was also one of the final blows to my marriage.

Florida and the start of the BDC

A new friend, Ron, who didn't know what was going on in my life at the time, became concerned for me. He knew the church was struggling, I stopped my business activities, and he saw my health

visibly declining. Out of the blue one day, he called me up, told me I needed a holiday, and he was going to take me to Florida.

Honestly, I didn't want to go. The thought of being on a plane and in airports with crowds freaked me out. The idea of having to make small talk and pretend that life was good was something I didn't think I had the energy to do.

When we got there, Ron bought a bunch of food and we got some great wine and cigars. For the first four days, I'd go to bed early and get up early; he would stay up late and get up late. We would get together mid-morning, cook, eat, hangout, talk about nothing, repeat. That was it.

For me at that time, it was surreal. He just wanted to hang out; he seemed to just like me as a person. I felt I didn't have anything to give, and he wasn't asking for anything.

I don't know how the conversation started. I can't even remember how I introduced the topic. I am sure it was like anything else I do in life, once I made I decision, I just ran at it full speed. By the end of our chat, on a windy beach in August, I had told him everything that I recalled at the time. My parents, the abuse, what I was struggling with, how my marriage and kids were suffering, and how I was tanked financially. I told him about how I couldn't control myself emotionally anymore, how I panicked, how I was fearful, and that I didn't know why.

At the end of it, about two cigars later, he said, "It stays with me. I'll never discuss this with anyone unless you bring it up with them when I am present." I knew I had taken a risk in trusting someone, but I also knew I couldn't keep trying to do this on my

own. I was dying on the inside. I felt like I was drowning and maybe, just maybe, I had been thrown a lifeline. As we walked back to the apartment it was like an incredible weight had lifted. I felt like I had not only unburdened myself, but that maybe I came across someone who might be prepared to help me carry my load for a little while.

Previously, when I told a few people my story, they ended up cutting off communications and treating me like a leper. It was like they couldn't cope or maybe they thought somehow the horrors that happened to me were going to infect them. Over the next couple of months, I waited to see if Ron's attitude towards me changed. It never did. I never questioned if he would discuss my story with others, I just noticed that he never brought it up.

One evening, I went around to Ron's house to have dinner with him and Alicia. Things were proving a challenge at home and I needed to get some input. As I opened up about what I was dealing with, Alicia looked lost. I had assumed Ron would have told her what we had discussed. In fact, I was comfortable with that idea, but he hadn't. I had to back track and fill her in on the daily issues I was facing. I remember the look in her eyes when I stopped; she was grieving for me. She grieved for what was done to me and for the ramifications it was having. She never pitied me, and in the years to come, she was never ashamed of me.

Roll the years forward

That fateful dinner took place on their back deck, and those two people are the foundational members of what I have referred to all through the book as the Back Deck Crew (BDC). The BDC

has been the reality check and wisdom council that has been my anchor all the way through my process.

Remember the trip to Atlanta and the brain scan that had such a positive impact on me? Ron and I were together. Ron was also the first person who told me that Melissa loved me. I said bullshit, he said I was wrong; the rest is history.

Remember the advice I got from a friend that said I needed to stop digging myself into a hole, and I should start by throwing the shovel out? That was Alicia. The friend who told me to make a list and prioritize what I need to work on, one thing at a time, for my recovery was Alicia again. She is also the custodian of "The Spoon" (you will read about that at the end of this chapter). It is Alicia and Melissa, who have been my daily reminders that the world is full of great and wonderful women whenever my head brings up the memories of so many others who have done me wrong.

That one decision on a beach in Florida to trust someone else was the smallest, largest decision that I have made to date. It is the decision that has had more impact on my journey than any other decision I have made thus far. This couple has known me at my worst and spoken to my greatness for nearly a decade now, and I love them for it.

The BDC today

One day I concluded that there was a high probability, and even a very firm likelihood, that I could quite possibly be in love with Melissa. I didn't know if this were true, as I was told for years that I didn't know what it was to love someone — that I was incapable of it, too selfish, too screwed up.

I honestly didn't know if I loved Mel. I enjoyed hanging out with her and doing stuff together. But this love and marriage thing didn't end so well the last time, and I didn't want to go through that again. I knew I still had a lot to work through, and I didn't want to burden or hurt anyone else, especially someone I cared about.

I concluded that if I did, in fact, possibly have deep romantic feelings for her of an everlasting sort, then there was also a tiny likelihood that I might even seriously entertain at some point in the not-so-distant future, entering into a long-term arrangement with her of a permanent nature.

When confounded with complex, unfathomable problems, I did what I always do: I got out a piece of paper and drew a chart (see Figure 7). This time it was different; this time I meant business; this time I devised a spreadsheet. (I can't believe I actually did this or that I am admitting to it. I am seriously embarrassed right now.)

To facilitate this little journey of discovery, I would take what I considered to be the finest piece of poetry on the nature of love that I had ever read, 1 Corinthians Chapter 13, and rate my affections against it to guage if I was truly ready to possibly be potentially serious in a long-term kind of way:

> *Love is patient and kind; love does not envy or boast; it is not arrogant or rude. It does not insist on its own way; it is not irritable or resentful; it does not rejoice at wrongdoing, but rejoices with the truth. Love bears all things, believes all things, hopes all things, endures all things.*

*Figure 7.* The Spreadsheet of Love

| Quality of Love | Do I feel this way, or can I do this? | My score on a scale of 1-10 |
|---|---|---|
| Love is patient | I can be patient with Mel. | 6 |
| and kind | I can be kind...got it. | 5 |
| does not envy or boast | Not an issue, I want the best for her. | 8 |
| it is not arrogant | I don't act proud around her. I'm humbled to be loved by her. | 9 |
| or rude | I can be but never deliberately. | 6 |
| does not insist on its own way | Hmm...tough one, I can be bossy. | 7 |
| it is not irritable | Sometimes she pisses me off. | 4 |
| or resentful | Don't have a problem in this area | 8 |
| it does not rejoice at wrongdoing | I never want to do wrong by her, but I know sometimes I do. | 7 |
| but rejoices with the truth | Always. | 9 |
| Love bears all things | I do my best, sometimes not so well. | 7 |
| believes all things | The best with her and for her. | 9 |
| hopes all things | Absolutely. | 9 |
| endures all things | I will. | 9 |
| | Score (out of 140) | 103 |
| | % Chance I'm in Love | 73.5% |

After working and reworking it, I concluded that I could in fact be approximately 73.5% in love. I needed to have a chat with the BDC before I went any further. My phone call went like this:

*"Hey Alicia, are you and Ron..*

*Yeah, no, good, good, yeah, well, you know,*

*What, sorry, yes I called you didn't I, well I was wondering if,*

*No, she is good yep, yeah great, they are fine as well.*

*Well you see I was wondering if you and Ron are around Friday? Oh today's Friday, right yes, I suppose today, are you here? I don't mean right here with me I am at home, I mean there, where are you? You're there aren't you?*

*What me, nothing's wrong,*

*Why would anything be wrong,*

*Are you okay? I'm great, how are you?*

*What?*

*You want to have dinner? That's a great idea, I was calling about that. When? Tonight? Friday?*

*I think I am around, yes I am.*

*Okay. Bye."*

*That went well*, I thought.

In preparation for dinner, I wrote out my spiel. It was about 8 minutes long. I printed it out, highlighted it, and practiced when and how to deliver my statistical revelation with the greatest impact.

Upon arrival, I decided that the welcome mat was not the appropriate place to bring up the topic. So I would wait, poised and prepared.

I tried to bring it up during the pre-dinner drink phase, but I nearly choked on a glass of Syrah.

I was determined to bring it up during dinner, but every time I tried, someone had already left the table.

After dinner, the air was filled with that tangible, somewhat awkward, *really not sure why we are here* feeling you find yourself in when someone calls you about something they say they need to talk about, but don't actually talk about it, and you really aren't sure why you are there thingo.

So I just launched. The whole spiel took about 4-1/2 seconds, and I sounded like a squirrel on caffeine, doing speed and not breathing.

"I know they told me I don't know what love is, but I came up with a matrix and I ran the numbers and I think it will work out, I am 73.5% sure I love her and I might actually think I want to marry her. Is that okay? Mel that is. Yes, I do, I think so. I'm pretty sure."

Well that's how I remember how the night went, that and Alicia laughing and saying, "You did the numbers?" while Ron went for more wine.

I never did get to show them the spreadsheet. They did, however, approve of Mel. Alicia's final words as she handed me leftovers were, "She's a good one, do right by her." I've tried to ever since.

Someone read the draft of this book and their reflection was that it sounded like everyone needs a Mel in their life if they are going to recover. I say yes, you do. And a Ron and Alicia. You can't do this alone, friend. Trust me, I tried.

## AFFLICTED OR INFECTED

May we live in peace without weeping. May our joy outline the lives we touch without ceasing. And may our love fill the world, angel wings tenderly beating.

—Irish Blessing

The past is behind, learn from it.
The future is ahead, prepare for it.
The present is here, live it.

—Thomas S. Monson

Learn to enjoy every minute of your life. Be happy now. Don't wait for something outside of yourself to make you happy in the future. Think how really precious is the time you have to spend, whether it's at work or with your family. Every minute should be enjoyed and savored.

—Earl Nightingale

Not Being the Second S in Keep It Simple Stupid

I know we all have things to deal with in our past, and I know we all have things we need to plan for in our future. These two areas get the majority of our attention. Often we spend so much time looking back, regretting, reminiscing, unpacking, rewinding, and even remembering that we forget our now, this day, today. At least I know I did. The road to my hell was not only paved with good intentions. I was carrying a backpack of guilt, pulling a cart of regret, followed by a mule train of condemnation. Emotional, relational and financial crap completely cluttered my life.

I was in Houston on business and was having a slow day, so I sat in my room watching TV. Nothing new was happening on E: Bruce Jenner was still Bruce, and Kim hadn't hooked up with Kayne yet. I was flipping channels aimlessly, and then I came across *Hoarders*. *Hoarders* is a reality TV show about people who would collect crap and keep collecting crap until their house/trailer/condo overflowed with crap. It was horrible, sad, awesome and a total train wreck. I couldn't look away.

The word *complicated* means difficult, confusing and involving many aspects. The word *clutter* means a disordered state or a bustle and confusion, or a heap, a pile, something that fills up and eventually takes over. Hoarders' lives got complicated and messy, not because of what they kept, but because of what they didn't throw out.

That night I took myself across the road to the Taco Garage and settled in with a quesadilla and a flight of mini-margaritas. As I was sitting, listening to the not so melodious warbling of a bald, Mexican/Asian hip-hop artist called Juan who went by the name of The Shaved Taco, I realized my life was no different than the people I saw on TV. My life wasn't simple; it wasn't straightforward. I was self-medicating through constant activity, always trying to push ahead, shoving more things in the front door of a very overcrowded emotional house. I was trying so very hard to get away from my past; I wasn't spending any time dealing with it. I was emotionally, spiritually and mentally cluttered.

In 1530, Jerome Weller wrote to Martin Luther complaining of despair and depressing thoughts. Luther wrote back saying, "Whenever the devil worries you with these thoughts, seek the company of men at once, or drink somewhat more liberally, jest

and play some jolly prank, or do anything exhilarating."[68] I could feel that I was on the edge of another epiphany; one that would probably involve me having to deal with the emotional hoard I carried around, so I ordered another flight of mini-ritas, cursed the devil and was a Lutheran for an evening.

Choosing my fruit

In May 2009, Shari Roan of the L.A. Times wrote in an article entitled, Bitterness as Mental Illness:[69]

"... that some psychiatrists are urging [bitterness] be identified as a mental illness under the name post-traumatic embitterment disorder. The disorder is modeled after post-traumatic stress disorder," she continues, "because it too is a response to a trauma that endures. People with PTSD are left fearful and anxious. Embittered people are left seething for revenge."

Roan quotes Dr. Michael Linden, a German psychiatrist and director at Linden Attention Learning Center in her article:

"[Bitter people]... feel the world has treated them unfairly, It's ... more complex than anger. They're angry plus helpless ... Embittered people are typically good people who have worked hard at something important, such as a job, relationship or activity. When something unexpectedly awful happens - they don't get the promotion, their spouse files for divorce or they fail to make the Olympic team - a profound sense of injustice overtakes them. Instead of dealing

---

68 W.H.T., "Luther Examined and Reexamined: A Review of Catholic Criticism and a Plea for Revaluation," 2015. HardPress

69 http://www.latimes.com/la-he-bitterness25-2009may25-story.html

with the loss with the help of family and friends, they cannot let go of the feeling of being victimized. Almost immediately after the traumatic event, they become angry, pessimistic, aggressive, hopeless haters."

Friedrich Nietzsche said, "Nothing consumes a man more quickly than the emotion of resentment."[70]

Stephen Diamond defines bitterness as: "A chronic and pervasive state of smoldering resentment; is one of the most destructive and toxic of human emotions."[71]

I think the best way to describe bitterness is that it's an emotional root[72] that if left untended, will grow like a weed and take over your life. This weed of bitterness grows inside of you because of your perception of an event, social ill, or personal wrong. This perception can become exaggerated or disproportionate over time, and if you allow it to take over your life, all you end up with is morbid hostility toward someone, something, or toward life itself.

*So here is the rub*: I could justify my bitterness.

I could justify my feelings of resentment towards Fred and Rosemary. I could justify my feelings of resentment towards many people who had turned their back on me when I needed them the most. When I told anyone my story, they told me I had

70 Nietzsche, Friedrich. "Why I Am So Wise," 2005. Penguin Books.

71 Diamond, Stephen A. "Can Bitterness Become a Mental Disorder?" Psychology Today, June, 2009. https://www.psychologytoday.com/blog/evil-deeds/200906/anger-disorder-part-two-can-bitterness-become-mental-disorder

72 Hebrews 12:14-15

a right to feel betrayed, upset, angry, and outraged. Maybe I did. But all of these things were cluttering up my soul, filling my mind, and distorting my future. I couldn't see past my memories anymore. My desire to be happy was looking more and more like a fantasy about happiness.

I was working around the house one day and cut my finger to the bone. What worried the doctor wasn't the injury, it was that I was about to get on a plane and spend a month in Israel riding camels and camping in the desert. He went to great lengths to tell me about the dangers of infection, loaded me with pills and creams and special swabs, and encouraged me to pee on my hand if necessary. He told me that if it got infected, I might not just lose my hand but my life.

Bitterness has the same potential. Affliction is something that happens to us; infection is something that happens inside us. When we dwell on the wrongs of the past, when we replay and recount the errors and lost opportunities, we are cultivating and feeding a root of bitterness. It is no longer an external thing, an affliction; it is an internal thing growing inside of us.

A root starts as a seed

Every plant starts as a seed, something small and nearly undetectable. Over time that seed germinates, and long before there is any physical sign on the surface of what is going on underneath, the roots have grown and are spreading out throughout the soil. The nature of the seed determines the nature of the plant. A good tree will produce good fruit, but a bad tree will produce bad fruit.

If you allow the seed of bitterness to take hold in your heart, it will grow an invisible root system that will spring up and impact not only your life, but also the lives of those around you. Something will set you off, and you will find yourself saying hurtful and harmful things that have nothing to do with the current situation. The infection has spread and eventually will pollute everything you touch, everyone you love, and everything you do.

## The thing with weeds

Have you ever noticed that weeds just seem to spring up over night? No one deliberately plants one. No one wants weeds, but if you're not paying attention to your garden, weeds just appear. Imagine that you have the best garden in the neighborhood — everything flourishing, everything in order — and then one night you come out and there is this weed standing in the middle of your garden mocking you. It's only one weed, a small weed, so you decide to leave it for now, to ignore it.

The first thing you find out about your weed is that it doesn't need tending. You won't have to fertilize your weed or care for your weed in any way whatsoever. In fact, the only thing you need to do for your weed to grow in the middle of your prize-winning garden is to ignore it. The second thing about your weed is that it doesn't matter how much you read about getting rid of it, how much you scream at it, pray over it, talk about it, or attend workshops on how to prevent it; it will just continue to grow. The only way to get that weed out of your garden is to physically remove it.

I never meant to get bitter. I never wanted to allow my afflictions to turn into an infection, but I had. By continually dwelling on what I had been through, I allowed the weed of bitterness to grow.

It wasn't only that I had neglected to root it out, but I felt I was actively feeding it. People could lie about me, hurt me, steal from me, but they didn't have the power to make me angry, jealous or bitter; only I could do that.

I realized I could not control my past or what was done to me, but I could control the impact of those things on my present and my future by controlling my present attitude. I concluded that an attitude was nothing more than a series of thoughts that I repeated over and over until they became a habit. The making or breaking of this habit, this attitude of mine, was completely under my control. If I could change my attitude about what happened in my past, then I could change my outcomes in the future.

## UNCLUTTERING MY SOUL

It is better to live in peace than in bitterness and strife.

—Confucius

Darkness cannot drive out darkness; only light can do that.
Hate cannot drive out hate; only love can do that.

—Martin Luther King, Jr.

The weak can never forgive. Forgiveness is the attribute of the
strong.

—Mahatma Gandhi

### Disclaimer

By now in the narrative, I am supposed to be astounding you with
my sheer awesomeness, heading towards wrapping it up with a
stunning conclusion and a breath-taking summary.

Sorry folks.

I'm still battling with bitterness and forgiveness even though
they are necessary for growth and forward movement. I know
forgiveness is a valuable quality and characteristic; it's just bloody
hard to do and some days I don't want to.

If what was done to me only affected me, then I would have been
able to move on long ago. If I had my time again, I never would
have married or had kids. The price they have to pay for Fred and
Rosemary's mindless, selfish indulgence is most days nearly too
much for me to consider. It would be easier if what were done
to me only affected me, but it doesn't. I still wake most nights

screaming. And my kids don't know what to think when they hear me at night, or find me in the morning sitting in my office, crying because of the nightmares.

I've come a long way, but I still have much farther to go. Each day I try and get a little bit better at it. I never try and get a whole lot better at it; I just try for 1% better at a time. If I can string 100 days together, then I'll be doing okay. Hell, I'd settle for 100 weeks at 1% a week. At this rate, it might be 100 years, but that is okay as well. I will be a better man than I am right now 10 years from now and that's all I'm shooting for.

Let's start with what I refer to as the 6 Myths about Forgiveness:

## Myth 1: It's easy; you just have to decide to do it.

<ROFL> Absolute and utter bullshit, not worth writing about. The people who say this sort of crap live in a bubble of narcissistic self-denial.

## Myth 2: Forgive and forget.

Ain't going to happen. Forgiveness doesn't mean forgetting. Neurologically, physiologically, emotionally, spiritually it cannot happen, nor do I believe it is meant to happen. If it were meant to happen, I wouldn't be sitting here writing to you about something that happened 50 years ago. I wouldn't remember it, but I do.

In 1985, Father Larry Jenco, a Servite priest, was kidnapped and taken hostage by terrorists in Beirut. Reflecting on his experience, he said:

*"Some people advise me to forgive and forget. They do not realize that this is almost impossible. Jesus, the wounded healer, asks us to forgive, but he does not ask us to forget. That would be amnesia.*

*I don't believe that forgetting is one of the signs of forgiveness. I forgive, but I remember. I do not forget the pain, the loneliness, the ache, the terrible injustice. But I do not remember it to inflict guilt or some future retribution. Having forgiven, I am liberated. I need no longer be determined by the past. I move into the future free to imagine new possibilities."[73]*

Real forgiveness acknowledges the offence and then makes the conscious decision to release the offending party from the consequences of it. A friend once described it to me like this, "Clearly seeing the offence; a person chooses to forgive and manifest this forgiveness by withdrawing the penalty of the offending action and continuing the relationship."

I believe this is true. For me this is my Gold Standard, what I aim for; what I am yet to achieve.

## Myth 3: Forgiveness means you're a doormat.

This statement may be true if you have a victim mindset. If you are *granting forgiveness* out of religious guilt or compunction,

73 Jenco, Lawrence Martin, O.S.M., "Lebanon Bound to Forgive: The Pilgrimage to Reconciliation of a Beirut Hostage," 1995. Ave Maria Press.

without any of the steps I am about to mention, then I believe you're setting yourself up for failure and will end up being considered a doormat by the people around you. There is a flipside to this doormat mentality, just like the Welcome/Go Away doormats I give people for Christmas. If you lean toward a victim outlook on life, then you'll probably be granting token forgiveness, while actively filling your bitterness bucket for later use.

Forgiveness is the last stage in a chain of events that starts with a slight misunderstanding or an argument over an action, point of view, or decision. You can't jump from argument to forgiveness without going through the checkpoints of confrontation, communication, understanding, reconciliation, and then rounding it out with a plan of agreement to move forward. At least two or three of these checkpoints have to be passed through before you can forgive which leads to the restoration of the relationship.

If forgiveness for you is simply giving someone a free pass without being prepared to discuss the issue, argument, disagreement, or hurt (perceived or real), you're going to destroy yourself, the relationship, or both. And yes, in that case, YOU are allowing YOURSELF to be a doormat.

## Myth 4: Forgiveness means you have to continue in a relationship with someone.

Who said? Forgiveness does not automatically mean reconciliation. They stole money from you, deserted you, stole your business, and lied about you. Do you want to stay friends with them? Why? Because you forgave them? That's not being nice; it's being stupid. Get up, dust off, confront, communicate and reconcile if that is what you want; or confront, communicate and move on if that is what you need to do.

## Myth 5: When someone asks you to forgive them, you have to.

No, you don't. Sometimes you should tell them they're a jerk.

Early on in my time in America, a guy I worked with in Australia for years heard of my success and became incredibly jealous. He somehow thought if he could ruin my reputation he could slip in and take my place. He deliberately used his position and influence, calling the business and church organizations I was contracted with, and lied about me. The result was it cost me hundreds of thousands of dollars in lost opportunities.

Six years later, I returned to Australia to attend a conference. One morning, I was having breakfast at the hotel surrounded by the Who's Who of this particular church denomination, and this guy spotted me. He came over very sheepishly and asked to sit down. In a very soft voice, he admitted to what he had done and how he felt terrible about it and wanted to ask my forgiveness.

In a very loud voice, loud enough to stop everyone else talking in the room, I recounted everything he had just said. I responded with, "You don't want forgiveness, you want to dump your emotional shit in my backyard so you can tick a box, feel good about yourself and move on. Ain't going to happen, Sunshine. If you want forgiveness, then I want to see repentance. I want you to call every person you lied to and acknowledge and admit what you have done. Then come back and apologize to me. Up until that point, you can go and fuck yourself."

The guy was a total dick and needed to be told he was a total dick. That sort of religious bullshit is why people lose sight of God and walk away from the church. Don't ever allow yourself to be manipulated into giving someone a free pass, particularly by people playing the God-card.

And what if he made the calls and told people he had lied about me and then called me to apologize? What would I have done then? I would have forgiven him, and we would probably still be friends today, because I like people who take responsibility for their crap. I'm also a firm believer in giving people a second chance, even if it's just to keep a close eye on them to see what they do in the future.

Now, all that being said, if someone approaches you with all sincerity, acknowledges they were wrong and is prepared to do what needs to be done to make it right - you're the dick if you don't accept the apology; your self-righteousness will come back to haunt you.

**Myth 6: When someone tells you they forgive you, they mean it.**

Sometimes or most of the time, but it can get complicated. If you truly have forgiven someone and truly have reconciled, then you should never feel the need to bring that particular incident/infraction up again. If the issue is not resolved, then you have to continue to communicate until a resolution is made. Only by being honest and self-aware can you give and receive real forgiveness.

If Melissa and I have an argument, and we have some doozies, we take however long we need to talk it over and get it right. Once we've worked through what we need to work through, we hold hands, ask for forgiveness, and receive it. That should be the end of it, but real life shows us that it is not.

Have you ever argued, done the "I forgive you" thing, and then found yourself wondering about something else that was said or

done and it starts the room spinning again? Conventional teaching says that you shouldn't bring the issue up again because you've already dealt with it. That doesn't work for us, particularly for me. Oftentimes what happens is that my brain will start to play things over and over again. My short-term memory will not recall that this issue was resolved. I start to wonder; I start to dwell on our argument and sooner or later I'll get anxious and paranoid as the deregulated *Fight or Flight Response* kicks in. If I don't find a way to stop the cycle, the whole issue we just resolved will spin up again, and I'll be in full fight mode about it.

I have trained myself that when I start to feel this happen, and while I can still remember the issue was resolved, I go for a walk. I think through, and literally practice out loud, what I am going to say to Mel when I get back to the house.

The conversation always starts the same:

"I need to talk about something you said the other day/this morning/last month, and I have been practicing how to say it."

The phrase "I have been practicing" is a cue to Mel that I am trying my best and I don't want to be hurtful or drag something back up. But I also don't want to leave something unaddressed that will end up getting out of proportion.

People with PTSD often need to do this. They need to talk about it over and over again until it gets settled once and for all in their mind and emotions.

Why is it like that for us? I'll try my best to explain it.

In an earlier chapter, I used an illustration about buckets to describe how memories crash into each other. I'm going to use a similar illustration here. If you have just randomly started reading at this point in the book, continue. If you've been reading it straight through, you can read this a second time or jump to the **.

Imagine that most people have different buckets for different emotions and situations. One bucket might be work, one family, one their past. An argument or a difficulty in one area of their life stays contained in that particular emotional bucket. When a person with PTSD stirs up internally, it's like a single bucket of emotions starts to vibrate. This vibrating bucket then starts to spill emotions over into other buckets. If things don't get slowed down internally, then the buckets start to crash into each other, and the swirling mass of conflicting internal emotional responses become an indistinct mess. The emotional buckets end up getting knocked over and spill into unrelated areas. That is why people who suffer with PTSD can seemingly go from 0 to 100 in a nanosecond - from calm to rage without any warning. This is also why something that starts as a concern in one area ends up being a rage in a seemingly unrelated area.

The worst thing someone like myself could hear at a time like that is, "Don't bring that up again, we have dealt with it, be a man and get over it." The thing is, I am not over it. In fact, I can't remember what started the swirl. I may not even fully remember that we have discussed the issue, or that we have dealt with it at all because my short-term memory is shorting out.

**That is why having a process in place like going for a walk and *practicing* a question or a response helps to deal with the swirl. By being allowed to revisit things that have been resolved, I can,

with reasonable calmness (normally I'll be running at about 50-70% elevation), bring out my concerns one at a time and talk about them again. By being able to step back into a discussion on the issue, I can be gently reminded of what we discussed, how we reconciled the issue, and what we decided to do to move forward.

This process may need to take place a couple of times about the same issue that arose during the same argument. The constant reassurance that things are okay, and that as a couple we have a plan, has enabled us to make forward movement together, instead of growing apart over time.

At the end of a *revisit* talk, Mel often reminds me that we talked all this over and we forgave each other. If there's a new issue discussed, we forgive each other for that issue as well. It takes time and effort. But we've found that by allowing ourselves room to go back over things, it's no longer taking me days and weeks to calm down, but hours and sometimes minutes.

Merely ignoring our memory of a grievance isn't forgiveness, it is the suppression of anger. Suppressed anger will fester, and the grievance will end up being used as a bully club in some future unrelated disagreement. That's not playing fair. Forgiveness has to be genuine and lasting, or over time suppressed anger will destroy your most important relationships.

Been there, done that, got the paperwork to prove it.

And now the 5 truths so you may walk in forgiveness and head towards wholeness:

**Truth 1: Forgiveness isn't a sign of weakness, but strength.**

About the same time I came to understand that forgiveness does not mean "forget-ness" is the time I came to accept that I didn't forgive people because I was weak, but because I was strong enough to do so. I realized that my ability to forgive was about who I wanted to be as a person, the greater value I was starting to place on my future, and the diminished power the past was having over me.

**Truth 2: You have to let go of the past to grab hold of the future.**

For me, the need to exercise forgiveness wasn't an emotional or spiritual decision; it was a practical one.

I noticed there were days where I would sit down to plan out my future, only to get up hours later, with the realization that all I had thought about was my past. I couldn't go on like that anymore. I needed to give myself permission to walk my path unhindered, not dragging old luggage filled with unforgiveness and bitterness along with me.

**Truth 3: To get whole, you have to make some hard relationship choices.**

We all know people who've had an unfortunate run in life - bad business decisions and relationship breakdowns, which have been beyond their control - these people need all the empathy and help we can muster. But then there is the other lot. They just seem negative by nature. They have an unsettling effect on you. Their negative emotions are often so intense, as they often talk about their circumstances and life in such a negative way, that just being around them will destabilize you.

When people found out I was in the middle of a divorce, they wanted to tell me their horror stories of lives and relationships ruined. They wanted to give me advice on what to do all based upon the wrongs they suffered at the hand of another. All this ended up doing was magnifying my struggles. I realized I was very susceptible to being swayed, not so much by the words of others, but by their moods and ways of thinking. I would fight hard to get into a good place emotionally only to be re-infected by the emotional struggles of others. By the very nature of forgiveness and bitterness, the people you associate with are critical. If you associate with people who infect, you will waste energy and time trying to extract yourself from the orbit of their emotional black hole.

I had to make choices, hard choices: BE AVAILABLE TO EVERYONE OR GET WHOLE.

## Truth 4: You need to understand your self-worth.

We are all wounded, and we are all inadequate; I know that is not unique to me. On a good day, the view of myself would vacillate between fragile and feeble. All I needed to push me over the edge was disapproval or rejection by those closest to me, be it perceived or real. I think one of the keys to move from bitterness into forgiveness was accepting that I was worth it. All of my life I was told I was of no value or I was only a good boy when I was performing to someone else's satisfaction. Combine this with the immense guilt I was feeling over hurting those I loved because of what I was dealing with, and I believed that I deserved to have a miserable future.

When you see yourself as having little value, you will feel the same about others. When you see yourself as not being worthy

of forgiveness, then you will feel the same about others. Once you start to change your view of yourself, extend mercy towards yourself for being imperfect and broken, then you'll do the same to other imperfect and broken people. You're screwed if you think you're perfect and have never made a mistake. You have condemned yourself to a cycle of perfectionism and performance anxiety that will manifest in a destructive downward cycle. But once you can accept that you are a broken human being trying to do life as best as you can, you can extend that grace to others.

## Truth 5: Dealing with dead people

Depending on your theology, you will either believe that the dead will be raised with the coming of Christ or at the coming of the Great Zombie Apocalypse. Neither of those two points of view will help you if the person you need to confront or seek forgiveness from is dead and you need resolution now.

My advice is to write it down. Get it all out. Make it detailed and specific. It may take months to write as bits and pieces come back over time. But once it's all out, then set a time and location to read it to them. It may be at a graveside or it may be in your backyard on the anniversary of their death. Whenever it is, make sure it's meaningful and memorable.

Once you have done that, burn it. Don't throw it in the trash or put it in your journal where you might re-read it. Destroy it. It is done. It is over. You have faced it, confronted them as best as you can, or you have asked for forgiveness, and now that part of your life is over. It's time to move on.

## MEL'S TURN

When John was probably the worst at dealing with his recall and had just begun gathering *tools* for his toolbox, he had one of those turning-point dinners with the BDC. He was explaining to Ron and Alicia how everything for him emotionally was connected. For example, if there were a bad day at the church office, particularly something emotionally charged that he had to handle, he couldn't help the wash that came and "sloshed his buckets" and affected other areas of his life. I believe he was finding that writing searing blog posts were a bit cathartic at the time.

Alicia's reflection was she understood that for John everything was interconnected, "Like a pot of stew," she said, "instead of a bento box." But with some of his blog posts, emails and conversations, it seemed like he had a huge spoon and was actively "stirring the pot." She said he wasn't helping himself cope with the sloshing, and that he should "give away the spoon."

I'm sure that was hard for him to hear, but he took that conversation to heart. He went home and after reflecting for a couple of hours, went to the kitchen and got a wooden spoon. On it he wrote, "I will not stir my pot. I will enjoy the journey." He took the spoon over to Alicia the next day and promised her that he would stop stirring the pot. That day, she became Guardian of the Spoon. It still sits in the pencil cup on her desk.

We all need friends who will tell us the truth, and who will walk with us as we endeavor to apply it. No matter how messy life gets, they help us sort it out over great food and bottles of wine, with tears and laughter.

**THE INFAMOUS SPOON**

## CHAPTER NINE

# Love and Other Bruises

Let's talk about sex, baby.

Let's talk about you and me.

Let's talk about all the good things

And the bad things that may be.

Let's talk about sex.

Let's talk about sex.

Let's talk about sex.

Let's talk about sex.

—Salt N Pepa

And when I get that feeling.

I want sexual healing.

Sexual healing, oh baby.

Makes me feel so fine.

Helps to relieve my mind.

Sexual healing baby, is good for me.

Sexual healing is something that's good for me.

—Marvin Gaye

## LET'S TALK ABOUT SEX

I stand before groups of people after the credits have rolled on the documentary, or at the end of a seminar, and I always say, "Ask me anything, and I will do my best to answer it."

Sometimes people ask questions about trafficking or abuse in general, sometimes they ask general questions about my childhood, sometimes about recovery. The questions they don't ask me in person, but always end up asking Mel or sending later via email, are often questions about sex. People don't want to ask me directly or publicly because they think it is too personal or that they're crossing a line they shouldn't be crossing.

In emails from other survivors or spouses of abused people, the question that comes up more than anything else now is how I have dealt with the issue of sex. They want to know about my attitude towards it: Do I still have it? Do I enjoy it? How did the abuse affect me? All of the questions have been valid and very sincere.

## A Survey

As I prepared to write this book, I knew I wanted to deal with the questions about sex. Because of the importance and the nature of the topic, I didn't want to base my writing solely upon my reflections or experience. So I prepared a simple survey and publicized it through social media. I was amazed at the response I received. Survivors were more than willing, even excited, to share their stories. Many told me that this was a conversation they felt was long overdue. Many said the topic of *The Sex Life of the Sexually Abused* felt like some "dirty secret" to be ignored, kept in the closet and not discussed. In other words, they felt the same feelings that surrounded their abuse, now enshrouded a very intimate and personal part of their adult life.

I set up the survey so it could be answered anonymously, and there were no *required* fields. I did it this way because I knew from my own experience that I would never put my name on something like this and be completely honest. I wanted people to feel safe so they could be open, transparent, and share only what they wanted to share.

## Respondents: 198

Males and females responded nearly equally. I think the men felt comfortable sharing because I was a man asking the question, and the women felt safe because I shared a similar experience.

The following is a summary of the questions asked:

*1) Name*

2) Do you or have you ever struggled with sex or intimacy in relationships in your post-abuse years?

3) If so, what sort of things have you struggled with?

4) Did you resolve those issues?

5) If so, what helped you or what did you do that brought resolution or closure for you?

6) Have you at any time felt you had sexual desires, needs or appetites that may not be considered normal by people who had not experienced abuse?

7) Have you been honest with your current or past partners about your sexual needs, desires, or struggles?

8) Do you still struggle with different areas of your sexuality?

9) Did you ever try to talk to your partner or someone else about your needs?

10) Were you able to resolve your differences or talk about your needs with your partner?

11) How was that received?

12) If it didn't go over well, how did you move forward?

13) What do you wish your partner knew about you, your past, or your sexual needs that you haven't yet told them?

14) Anything else you think would help other people?

15) Would you like to give your email address to receive a summary of the results when they are finalized?

## A summary of responses

What I would like to do for you is paint the overall picture of the effect of sexual abuse/trafficking on people and how it has impacted their sexuality and sexual desires/practices.

## What types of abuse were experienced?

The responses covered just about everything you could imagine. Trafficking, homosexual rape, heterosexual rape, incest, gang rape. Abuse that was a single event to abuse that lasted years. The abusers/traffickers were both male and female, family members, friends, and strangers.

## What were the long-term effects of the abuse?

Every person spoke of an effect in their personal life that they could track back to the abuse. Not one of the respondents said there was no aftermath from their abuse experience. Most still feared, or battled with, physical and/or emotional connectedness. Some battled rage and anger. Some had succumbed to substance abuse as a way of coping.

## Do you have an interest in sex?

There emerged two very distinct camps or responses to the series of questions I asked about sex. There's a stereotype that people who have been abused have no interest in sex and derive no pleasure from sex. This stereotype did not hold true.

95% of people said they had sexual desires that did not fall within societal norms. Many described struggling during sex with triggers

and flashbacks of past abuse. They found these challenging to deal with, but all who figured out a way beyond them did so through open and honest communication with a trusted partner.

## Group 1: No interest in sex as a result of abuse

Approximately 45% of people talked about not having an interest in physical intimacy - everything from touch to intercourse was a challenge for them. They all said they would like to, but they just can't at this stage in their recovery.

Some have not had a sexual relationship of any sort. Of those who did, many were unable to orgasm. They found sex a chore, not a joy. It was something they felt compelled to participate in because they knew it was important to their partner.

Many also felt dirty or soiled if they ever engaged in sex, either casually or in a long-term relationship.

Very few people in this group felt able to communicate what they struggled with and why. This lack of communication caused strain, and in most cases, led to the ultimate destruction of primary intimate relationships. Both men and women struggled in this area.

## Group 2: Very interested in sex

The remaining 55% would describe themselves as hypersexual and would have what they consider an abnormal need for sex. Within Group 2, 25% talked about having sexual fantasies and desires they felt they could rarely or never discuss with their intimate partners.

The people in this group had desires and responses that were far ranging. Many felt they were not supposed to like sex because of their past experiences. Many felt their needs and appetites were too strong or perverted to mention them - even to those that they trusted and who professed to love and care for them. Often when they tried to talk about their needs to their partners, they were met with skepticism, and at times even ridiculed. As a result, they either moved on from the relationship or never brought the topic up again. Again this struggle is not gender-based.

There was a recurring need in this group to engage in fantasy role-play. Their fantasies included rape re-enactment, BDSM, and sexual games that focused on being in control of their partner or being controlled by their partner. These responses were not gender-specific, but I did notice that the majority of female respondents seemed to desire being controlled by their partners. They stated they wanted to let go with someone they trusted not to harm them.

I mentioned this because it can seem counter-intuitive. It is also contrary to much of the literature and conversations that happen in therapy circles. Up until 2013, BDSM was considered a dangerous practice and an activity of sexual deviants;[74] yet many within this sub-culture actually scored better on many indicators of mental health than those who didn't practice BDSM.[75]

Of the few in Group 2 who were able to role-play with a trusted partner, they mentioned getting closure on issues that had affected

---

74 http://www.sexhealthmatters.org/news/bdsm-and-psychological-health

75 http://www.huffingtonpost.com/2013/06/05/bdsm-better-mental-health-study_n_3390676.html

them since the abuse event took place. I don't know if this happened because they overwrote painful experiences with positive ones; if they experienced control when they at times felt helpless; or if they were controlled in a manner that wasn't threatening and they simply enjoyed it. In the reading I did after the survey results came in, I found a range of anecdotal articles that alluded to all three of these being true.

## General Questions

When given an opportunity to pass on any personal advice to other survivors, the participant responses were very moving. Nearly all spoke of the need to pursue forgiveness. They said the ability to forgive those who hurt them was essential to them heading toward wholeness. Some still found this difficult, yet all knew it was important.

Nearly all respondents talked about the need to *forgive themselves*. They had done things they regretted; and had hurt others, while they tried to come to terms with their experience. They were all desperate for a sense of inner peace.

In the last part of the survey, I asked respondents to add a comment, any comment they'd like me to pass on to you. They said things like, "Please listen to us," "Please be patient with us," "We are struggling, but we are trying," and "Don't judge us."

They all recognized this would be a lifelong journey of recovery for them, and they wanted to have someone to walk with them towards wholeness.

## THE POWER OF A PARTNER

And a heart

Is not a stone

And is fragile

When alone

By my side

By my side

Won't you be by my side

—Ben Harper

Melissa has never known me *well*; or she never knew me before I got sick. She has seen the worst of me, while having nothing else to compare it with to give her some hope that I could be anything different than a man struggling.

For many years we worked together in a business capacity and became friends. When the nature and depth of our relationship changed, she never once called me ill, or thought of me as less of a man, or not good enough for her. She always talked about a future time and place when she believed I would know peace, and together, we would know happiness.

At times in business meetings when I would stutter, or I would start to panic, she would calmly step forward and take over until I could center myself again. She always covered my challenges from the scrutiny of others; never once did she expose a weakness. She is fiercely protective like that; she would never allow others to think poorly or speak badly of me. She has never used my

struggles as a leverage point for personal manipulation or to degrade me or make me feel small about myself.

<u>I see you.</u>

A phrase that she often uses with me when I am struggling is, "I see you." This has come to mean so much to me. She sees me. She sees me struggle, she sees me fail, she sees me succeed, she sees me trying - she sees ME, all of me.

That term has also come to mean a lot to her. When the days are difficult, when the nights are full of irrational fears, when the arguments are filled with accusations of things she has never done or maybe never even knew about, I hear her say "I see you." They might be the same words, but her tone is different. She may say them in my direction, but she is saying them to herself. I hear her reminding herself to look beyond the broken/crying/panicking 11-year-old boy fighting for his life, and see the 54-year-old man trying to claw his way back to reality.

My struggle doesn't diminish me in her eyes, in fact it makes her proud. She is proud of me. Proud of how hard I try. Proud that I am growing and becoming whole, proud that I don't ever give up, and she knows that I will never quit.

<u>I didn't marry a caregiver.</u>

A good definition of a caregiver is a person who provides direct care, as for children, the elderly, or the chronically ill. They spend a lot of time and emotional energy making sure the frail, or the infirm, or the immature are safe and comfortable in life. As a man, there is nothing more degrading and debilitating than

to see your wife and best friend taking the role of a caretaker. I know I can't do things other men can do, or even that I used to do. I know I am not who I used to be. I don't need my wife, my life partner, to step in and pretend she is some mother figure caring for a hopeless, helpless child.

I know this is hard for some couples, particularly couples who have to try and deal with PTSD at a midpoint in a relationship. If this attitude is allowed to creep into a marriage, then the marriage is in danger. A man gets married because he wants to spend his life building a life with his best friend. When his best friend moves from the role of partner to caretaker, she changes the dynamic of the relationship in a way that is unnatural and not tenable. *Let me put it this way:* mothers are caregivers, and you can't make love to your mother. I don't know how to put that in a way with the genders/roles reversed, but you get the point.

There are definitely times when Melissa cares for me. There are even times when she might have been called my caregiver by others outside of our relationship, but this was never a title or role she sees herself having. She loved a man, married a man, and has never seen me as anything else but her man.

Mel has told me time and time again that when she looks at me, she doesn't see a broken man; she sees a man doing the best he can with what he has, and that gives me three things:

1) It means I can trust her. I don't believe she will leave me or turn her back on me if I have a rough day/week/month/year.

2) It gives me the courage to face whatever I am facing on whatever day it is, head on with full force. And I know that if I fail, she will celebrate my effort and not my mess.

3) It fuels my determination to get up every day and do everything I can to be the very best me I can be.

Communication, Sex, and Money

Many years ago I was sitting with an older, wiser friend and he casually stated that he believed all the marriage issues between men and women could be classified as problems with either money, sex or communication.

Mel and I have come to understand that communication is the basis for all of life. We see our day-to-day scheduling and discussion of how I am doing or what I am struggling with, and what we need to be doing to make life easier for both of us, as an issue of communication. We don't communicate because I have a *need* or I am *needy*; we communicate because we are best friends and want to help each other succeed.

Since John-A-Geddon and the divorce, things have been very tight financially. Everything, from the loss of income to finding a job in the initial stages that allowed the flexibility I needed, was a challenge. When I was preparing the paperwork for the divorce, I had a gut feeling that I wanted to pay off the original family home and all of the credit cards and car loans associated with my first relationship. I wanted to do this for two reasons. The first reason was because I committed to taking care of someone for life. Even though the marriage fell apart because of an *illness*, I didn't feel that released me from the obligation I made to her and

her father. The second reason was because I never wanted my children to be fearful they wouldn't have a roof over their heads. This meant I'd only get about 20% of what I was entitled to by Texas Law and would start from scratch financially.

Melissa's response to all of this was, "Whatever is going to help you sleep at night with the knowledge you have done your best." She was a firm believer that I would not only find my feet again, but my later years would be more impactful and financially rewarding than my earlier years.

And we lived happily ever after. <ROFLMAO>

Then the movie, travel expenses, new mortgage, educational needs of the kids, medical expenses, dishonest business partners, and so it goes on. We didn't have a lot when we started out, and we certainly couldn't afford a lot. We got rid of car loans, bought second-hand vehicles, eliminated all the recurring debt that we could, while at the same time getting as many credit cards as we could (at 0% interest) in case things got tough. We budgeted and hung on to each other and Mel's belief that it would all work out in the end.

Through it all we talked, we juggled, we laughed, and we had a lot of great date nights - a pizza, Netflix, and great sex. Great breakfast meetings - toast, coffee, and great sex. Great lunch meetings - a fresh salad, great sex - there is a bit of a theme here. Even if the world was going to hell in a hand basket, and we didn't know if we would have the money we needed for tomorrow, or if tomorrow would be a difficult day for us, we had the here and now and we squeezed everything we could out of it.

<u>Sex is a conversation - have you talked to your best friend today?</u>

Have you ever had those times when you're arguing with your partner, and you're walking around the house trying to avoid each other and not say anything? Horrible aren't they? It's so tiring trying not to communicate.

After we had one of those days, we were lying in bed after having awesome make-up sex. Mel rolled over and said something like, "I think sex is a conversation and I like talking to you. We should talk more often."

I said, "I need at least 30 minutes before I talk to you again."

We have discovered that sex is the most intimate communication that we can have with each other. Some days our conversations are funny, other times raunchy and rough, others quiet and calm – and so is our sex.

We saw sex as the gift we gave each other that no one else on earth would ever share. It was never a tool used against the other person. We have never withheld sex. We have always discussed it, and we thoroughly enjoy it at least once a day.

<u>Our perspective became our reality.</u>

Early on I came up with a couple of definitions that helped me put a handle on what I was dealing with. If a panic attack or a flashback happened and I managed to contain it or bring it under control but was still feeling de-regulated, I called that an *incident*. An *incident* was something that when it happened, it only affected me. But, if I were triggered and unable to stop the

Standing there,
holding each other
as close as our own skin...
looking at our future,
not sure what it held.

It was large
and full of equal parts
danger and adventure,
and we wanted it all.

Meme created by Dr. John A. King, originally published at drjohnaking.com.
Photo by Patrick Fore on unsplash.com.

emotional escalation in time with my fear, panic, and behavior starting to affect the people around me, I called that an *episode*.

I hated that what was done to me as a child not only affected me as an adult, but also all of those around me. *Incidents* I could cope with; but *episodes* left me devastated for days feeling guilty, remorseful, and discouraged.

I might be having a good day or a good week, to only have something trigger an incident or episode, and I'd feel like I lost the ground I was trying to reclaim. Mel and I came up with a new way of talking about these challenges. If something happened, once it calmed down, we would talk about the great day I had with a painful hour in the middle; or the great week with the one challenging day; or the great month with the rough week. I went from being a continual loser to a continual winner with the odd hiccup. As I mentioned earlier, I might fall, but I was always falling forward – it was all a matter of perspective. This simple change to how we approach our life gave me permission to fail, get up, and go again.

I know without a shadow of a doubt that without her loving reassurance, I would not be as far down the track towards wholeness as I apparently am. This phenomenon is what I call THE POWER OF A PARTNER. Partnership isn't ignoring the flaws and faults in another; it is looking beyond those faults and believing for the best.

## RANDOM QUESTIONS FROM RANDOMER FRIENDS

Love and other bruises didn't have to choose us.

But it did and I'm alive and I'm trying to survive.

—Air Supply

Cause I'm, I'm friends with the monster that's under my bed.

Get along with the voices inside of my head.

You're trying to save me, stop holding your breath.

And you think I'm crazy, yeah, you think I'm crazy.

—Eminem

Over the last few years, I've been asked a lot of questions — some embarrassing, some provoking, some insulting, and some insightful. As we started towards the final editing stages of this book, I wanted to make sure I was answering the questions people would want answered; questions they might want to know about me; or questions that might help them in their journey towards a better and brighter future.

Instead of trying to manufacture questions people might have for me, I asked some of my friends for theirs. Some of these people have known me for years and know the whole story, so they based their questions on what they think might help others. Others know parts of my story and their questions gave me insight into things I haven't addressed thus far.

When I looked at these questions, they brought back the memories I overcame and didn't even think about anymore. Other questions reminded me that I'm still trying to work them out. I thought it might be interesting and/or helpful to you if I included them within this book, as they were sent to me, with my attempt to answer them.

## QUESTIONS ABOUT MY PARENTS:

*In the future do you have plans to see them and make them a part of your life?*

No. They won't take responsibility for their actions, so I don't see that there is a way forward.

*Does society's thinking of "they must be punished for what they did" create conflict within you?*

There are always consequences for actions. What they did wasn't right, the thought of them getting punished for what they did neither brings me joy or anguish. I firmly believe that they will reap what they have sown, and I spend very little time (if any) nowadays thinking about them.

*Since you are a really good man, what were the good things they taught you?*

I don't think I am a good man. I think I am a man trying his best, but my opinion of myself isn't that high. Mel says I am good and Alicia says I have come a long way — I trust them.

My mother got pregnant early. I believe she was attempting to force my father into marriage to get out of the small town where they grew up. When abortion was mentioned to them as an option, they decided not to. For that I am grateful.

*Do you think they (your parents) came from similar abuse, or do you think it was something new to them? Do you think they have changed?*

From what I know, they both came from difficult backgrounds. They have used their experiences to justify their behavior. I don't think that is acceptable.

I have never abused my kids. My kids have been disciplined, spanked on their bottoms, grounded, sent to their rooms, had their bedroom doors removed or light bulbs taken out, but never abused.

I don't have any contact with them to know if they have changed. My last experience with them would suggest they had not.


## GENERAL QUESTIONS

*Does "Time heal wounds?"*

Wound healing is an interesting analogy. Part of the process of healing is similar to how the body gets rid of any foreign object. Often this includes infection and ultimately an eruption as the body cleanses itself. The wound either closes itself or it has to be closed. This process results in a scab and a scar. Any scar tissue

has to be massaged and worked for full movement to be restored to the body part.

I believe what happened in 2008 was my mind purging the repressed memories that had been causing a mental/emotional infection. It has taken years of cleaning and caring for the wounds for healing to take place. I am at a stage of trying to massage or work the old scarred areas to get full motion back.

Wounds heal, but scars remain. I have come to see my scars not as ugly blemishes, but as medals of Honor. They catalogue my journey, like an internal tattoo. My story no longer brings me embarrassment or shame, like old, red-bloated scars sometimes do. I am allowing myself to rejoice in my tenacity and resilience. On my worst days, I can look at my *medals* and say, "You bastards didn't kill me. I survived. I win."

*Before the day of your movie-reel-like breakdown, and aside from any other fragmented flashbacks, did you have any other signs that something was off kilter? Was there any behavior you displayed or decision-making that seemed strange or extreme that you would now attribute to the abuse you suffered?*

Yes. My *incidents* or *episodes* didn't start in 2008; I believe I have had them all of my life. Looking back, I think they happened maybe once a year or once a quarter. As I got older and the pressure of life, business, ministry, and marriage started to apply itself, they seemed to increase in frequency and intensity. The behavior was so abnormal back then that it caused great confusion and relationship strain, particularly in my first marriage. I didn't know what was wrong, and just put it down to me having to grow up and change and not be such a dickhead.

When the meltdown happened, I now had the *why* to the *what* that was occurring on a weekly and sometimes daily basis.

*What triggers your flashbacks?*

A trigger is something that transports someone back to an event or brings up a memory of the original trauma. They are tough to predict. Over time, I have learned that certain things have a tendency to bring back memories, and I either avoid them, or I have developed ways to cope with them.

Smells are a big one for me. If a washing detergent reminds me of my childhood, I can't stand to sleep on the sheets or use the pillow. Strong odors like incense when you walk into a house or a shop take me back to parties and events instantly.

Movies or songs, or even places or activities can be triggers. If I am in a room or a location that is overcrowded, I get fearful and panic-ridden. I feel like I'm trapped and cannot escape.

*How do you control your anger against those who you know are currently involved in abusive behavior towards children?*

I take a deep breath and pray that God will cause their body to be infected with boils and that their genitals fall off.

*How do you respond to those who say that if God were real, He wouldn't let this happen to children?*

I remember one night as a kid crying myself to sleep, feeling desperate and alone. I dreamt that God sat beside my bed all night and I held His hand. When I woke up, my hand was hanging off

my bed. It was like I was gripping His index finger like a little child holds the hand of His father. At that point, I knew that He was with me through it all, that I wasn't alone and He cared for me.

We live in a world that is filled with good people and bad people and people who delight in destroying something beautiful, just because they can.

God didn't rape me. God never abused me. God never left me. I believe He was grieved by all that happened and never wants anyone to go through what I experienced. People chose to hurt and abuse me, not God.

What He has done for me is turn all things around for good. I would not be the man I am today without what I have been through, and I like who I am becoming.

*Most importantly, when do you want to have a cigar with your best mate?*

I'll see you Wednesday at 4 P.M. after my meeting downtown, but I am short on cigars, I'll need to bum one. Love you Ron.

*What practices, exercises, and types of therapies are needed?*

There is a range of different therapy methods and therapists. None are perfect, and none are a cure-all. I believed that I was responsible for my recovery and that therapy was simply another tool in my toolbox. It was *part of* my solution, not the solution.

*Is it, do you think, possible to be fully healed from abuse? Rarely? Almost never? Often?*

I don't think you ever fully *heal*. I have come to believe that what you do is get better at managing yourself and your condition. Drugs don't cure it; therapy doesn't cure it; prayer doesn't cure it; all of these things are tools in the toolbox. But if you are not actively seeking new tools and using them, then you will never grow towards wholeness.

*Who were your good influences?*

Over my lifetime I have had the pleasure of working with and knowing some exceptional people. None of them were perfect, no one individual I would call a father or mentor, exclusively. My attitude is that life is a smorgasbord, not an a la carte menu. I have learned to graze off the experience and wisdom of others; assimilate the good and tasty morsels of their lives; and leave the Brussels sprouts to others. (I believe there is a solid theological argument that Brussels sprouts only grew in the garden after man fell from grace.)

I read a lot. Every book I read, be it fiction or non-fiction, I try to take away a life lesson or something I can apply.

*How did your experience affect your teen years, and your 20's and 30's? What effect did it have on your career path?*

I am not sure how, but I think it must have. I know I was often lonely and felt isolated, and was prone to depression. At college, I passed out drunk and woke up being molested by a staff member and a fellow student. I look back at things like that, and I realize that brokenness attracts brokenness. I must have allowed myself to be in places or relationships that were not safe.

In my 30's and with starting a career I don't think I chose wisely. I was looking for a place to belong, desperate for acceptance and I ended up in business relationships that were very totalitarian.

I don't think going into the ministry was the best thing for someone who had my underlying issues. Constantly dealing with the emotional needs of others was very taxing and stressful. There were personalities in the organization where I worked that were spiritually abusive and emotionally manipulative. Again, I think I attracted those sorts of people - all the way into my 50's. When I turned 50, I think I just ran out of "give-a-fucks" and walked away from relationships that were hurtful and not helpful.

*Did you ever want to give up?*

I think that I am, by and large, a positive person with a positive outlook.

I can't remember ever wanting to give up. I mentioned coldly contemplating suicide on a couple of occasions. It wasn't that I wanted to end my life; I just wanted to stop hurting those I loved. I knew I couldn't do it overnight like they wanted or needed me to. In the end, my decision not to give up was based on not liking to lose; WHILE I HAD BREATH, I STILL WANTED TO FIGHT.

*How did you get out of that stage and into a more positive, one foot in front of the other, space?*

When I started to try and answer some questions for myself, I couldn't find any books or resources for men dealing with sexual abuse. So what I did was break down the areas that I was battling, and start to research solutions for those. I knew I had issues with

anxiety, mood swings, and depression, so I began to research and read about each of those individual areas and outlined suggested solutions. I understood my body, mind, and spirit was a complex system that was interrelated and interconnected.

I looked at the commonalities that these solutions presented, a bit like a very complicated Venn diagram, identified core issues that affected everything, and set to work on those first. Key components were the endocrine system, the role of diet and exercise, the ability of color to alter mood, and the role of positive confessions and meditating on positive things.

I remember one day reading the parable Jesus taught about the mustard seed; how out of the smallest seed grows the biggest tree. I came to understand that instead of taking oak-sized steps, I should focus on *seed-sized steps*. This realization permitted me to attempt to succeed at small things on a daily basis, which I knew over time would have big impacts.

*If you get depressed, what works to bring you out of it now?*

First, I examine my diet and exercise regime. Have I been doing what I know to do, or have I been eating cookies and sleeping in? Next, I look at my schedule to see if I've been cramming too many things in like John 1.0 tended to do. I know that John 2.0 needs to live at a slower pace to stay balanced and upright - a little bit like those air-filled punching bags or knock-down toys we had as kids.

And then, believe it or not, I change the color of my shirt and the music I listen to. I went through a stage where all I would wear were Superhero T-shirts. People thought I was just going

through some weird phase of not dressing well. I wasn't - it was deliberate. In fact, at the first screening of the film in L.A., I wore a Star Wars T-shirt. I told everyone that it was because it was May 4; it wasn't. I wore it because it made me feel strong and invincible. People were focused on something other than me, and it gave me a conversation piece. I know that might sound weird to others, but to me, it is just another piece of my puzzle; a tool in my toolbox that helps me when I recognize my world is topsy-turvy.

I also wore colorful Chucks with expensive suits for many years for the same reason; but they started to hurt my feet.

*What are a few must have, daily practices that keep you positive and on the right track?*

Bible before breakfast, normally with a coffee and cigar. I follow that by about 30 minutes to an hour of a leadership book or TED talk or video.

I like going to the gym around 3 in the afternoon. That is when my metabolism is down, and I am prone to introspection for some reason.

I try to avoid sugar and processed food. I eat a mostly plant-based diet. I limit my use of alcohol. I take very few prescription medications. I don't do recreational drugs; never have. I am, however, very interested in the work being done with the use of medical marijuana and the treatment of PTSD. I am not sure if I would ever use it; the thought of being drugged and vulnerable is too much for me right now.

I spend time with people I care for and whom I know care for me. Friends who know all my crap and shortfalls and still like me despite myself. The list is short but the company is good, and I really look forward to seeing them.

I don't give too much of a damn anymore about what others think. That's an important daily practice, but challenging if you have never met me before.

*Part 1 - What is your greatest gift to others today?*

I enjoy taking complex issues, breaking them down, and making them accessible to people.

If I walk into a store to buy something, and the salesperson or technician makes it sound like it is so incredibly complicated that only they know how it works, I ask to speak to someone else who knows the product. Why? It doesn't matter what it is; it's only complex if you haven't taken the time to understand it.

I want to do that for the issues of abuse, human/sex trafficking, and dealing with and overcoming PTSD.

*Part 2 - What do you think it will be next year?*

The current model for identifying victims of human trafficking and abuse was created in the late 80's early 90's. So many things have changed since then. I believe it's time for us to update and equip our law enforcement, health care professionals, and community groups with tools and training that will make their jobs easier. It's a complex issue, but I'll beat it.

*What are your dreams for yourself, the world, youth, and children?*

William Wilberforce was the catalyst for the end of the slave trade in the British Empire. Three days before his death, the British Parliament passed the Slavery Abolition Act of 1833, which abolished slavery in most of the British Empire. If one man can make that much of a difference in his generation, what could millions of us do today?

I don't think I could spend my next few years doing anything better for my children than toiling to create a world where they and their children were free from the fear of slavery and exploitation.

## MEL'S TURN

I was so surprised by the number of responses to the sex survey. I hope that some of what we've been able to share will help others. I can say that vulnerability (especially in the bedroom) requires tremendous bravery. Any time John is willing to be open enough to share his needs or desires with me, I consider it a precious gift. I do my best to treat it with great respect. I believe we've only scratched the surface of what intimacy can be, and I look forward to what the future holds for us.

It is a grand adventure we're on. In any relationship, there comes a depth with some uncertainty and trials, and we are in the midst of creating some depth, John and I. As he mentioned, we've had some *financial creativity*, as I like to call it. One hundred years from now, that won't matter. What will matter is how well we loved each other, how we brought out the best in each another, and the difference we make in the lives of others.

One thing that is certain, we are committed to the journey. We are committed to the wonderful process of getting to know one another better each day, laughing, and doing life together.

# EPILOGUE

# What's Next?

Frequently I am asked, "What's next for John and Mel? What is the big picture for you both?"

I don't know really. I could tell you I have a 5/10/15 year plan to stop abuse, to end human trafficking, and save the universe. Maybe even bring peace to the Middle East and North Korea in a Dennis Rodman sort of way, but then that would be BS. It's not that I don't have some dreams, and even goals and plans, it's just that John 2.0 is still very, very new for both of us. To be honest, I never imagined a future like the one I am currently inhabiting.

So instead, I'll tell you a story that was given to me one day by the one person who has always been closer than a brother to me, and more of a father than anyone I have ever known.

## THE RAFT AND THE SPEEDBOAT

The old man stood on the boat dock with his grandson, a passionate wild-eyed young man in his 20's, looking out over the tranquil hills and valley that surrounded the farm. A stream running between the hills feed the vibrant lake year-round on its way to the ocean many miles away. Tethered to the dock was a 1948 Chris Craft runabout he had painfully restored years ago. Next to it was a six-man inflatable raft similar to the one that the old man's father had used in World War II.

They both stared at the runabout. The boy knew the stories were about to start and they did. How he had courted Grandma in it; how all the kids learned how to water ski; and the time his sister Bethany won the State Championship. The boy smiled quietly as his Granddad talked, knowing that the only reason he probably didn't sell the boat was because he enjoyed pissing off "all them fancy new neighbors from town who just came up for the weekend, bloody tree huggers." Before she died, his mother said they were very much alike, and he was starting to believe she was right.

He missed her and Dad, badly; often; especially this year as he headed off to college. He moved in with Granddad the same week the accident happened. Grandma had died the year before, and as he looked back, he realized them living together had probably saved them both.

"What's with the raft, Granddad?" he asked.

Taking him by the hand, like he was still only 8, he turned and started leading them back toward the house. "Did I ever tell you

about the time your Grandma and I took the river all the way to the coast?"

"No. Really? That would have been a blast."

"We certainly did. Now let me think, it was Grandma, Bill and Susan Thomas, before they were married and George and Betty Mueller, before they had kids."

Granddad settled into his favorite chair and started to pack a pipe.

"Took us four days. The river was high, and we had a lot of snow that year, and the water was bloody cold. I remember when Susie fell in on the second day; she nearly turned blue. Your Grandma offered to dry her clothes over the fire. To give Susie some privacy, all us boys headed back down to the river to smoke and have a beer. We are about halfway there, and Bill tells us he forgot his pipe and turned back to go get it."

Suddenly he rocked back in his chair and started to laugh the way an old man laughs when he knows the best part of a familiar story is coming up.

"Suddenly we hear the girls screaming and yelling like they were under attack, so we turned right around and started running back towards camp. Well, George, he ran for college, so he sprinted way ahead of me. There I was following behind him. I rounded the bend in the track just in time to see Susie run out of the bush, butt naked, not one stitch on her. She runs out onto the path like she was being chased by a Bear and BOOM, she runs straight bang into George, knocking him to the ground. Then out of the

blue, here comes Bill hurtling down the track, running for his life yelling, 'I didn't see nuthin!' being chased by your Grandma.

Apparently, when Bill had gone back up, he tried to be sneaky and get into his tent without disturbing or embarrassing Susie. Well, that just didn't work out so good. Susie was taking the last of her gear off and heard something in the bushes. She turned around and saw Bill sneaking by. She lets out this mighty scream. Bill looks up at Susie. Your Grandma looks up and sees Bill standing there staring at Susie and figures he has come to get an eyeful before the wedding, and she starts a-yelling. Susie starts screaming some more, bends down and picks up the only bit of clothing not hanging over the fire, two wet socks, and runs straight past Grandma and into the bushes at full steam. Grandma turns and starts running at Billy."

Granddad is rocking back and forth in his chair faster and faster, trying to catch his breath between laughs.

"Betty told us later that when Susie screamed, Bill looked up and just stood there his eyes as big as saucers looking at Susie in all her glory, mesmerized, like a deer in headlights.

Betty said Bill seemed to come around when he heard his name being screamed and looked up to see Grandma hurdling the fire and running at him. Apparently, he turned right around and started running for his very life back down the path yelling 'I didn't see nuthin.' I didn't see nuthin!'"

The old man is lost; laughing, crying, re-living, re-smelling, retelling the story while the boy sits, knowing he is hearing something very special, almost sacred.

"So, anyway, I round the bend just in time to see Bill being chased by your Grandma, trip and fall right on top of George and butt-naked Susie. But here is the funny part..."

He was laughing so hard he could hardly breathe.

"Your Grandma was so close behind Bill, she didn't see the pileup and didn't have time to stop. As Bill trips, she follows him to the ground, her dress flies up over her head - and here is the thing, the thing is, SHE DIDN'T HAVE ANY PANTIES ON!"

He rocks so far back in his chair, roaring with laughter, the boy thought he was going to tip it over, and the fancy neighbor across the lake comes out on his deck to investigate what all the racket is about.

The boy jumped to his feet howling with laughter. "MY GRANDMA!?"

Crying and breathing hard he squeaks out:

"I know, she had sat in some water earlier, and she was drying them over the fire as well. So anyways, I come around the corner, and this is what I see. George is on his back; Susie is face down on George; Bill is on his back lying on top of Susie, and Grandma's hiney is shining in the moonlight!

Looking out over the lake, brushing pipe tobacco off his work pants, he muttered longingly to himself, "That woman had such a nice arse."

He straightens himself in his chair and with words laced with false chivalry, he launches back into the story.

"Well, I did the only thing a real man would do to protect his woman's honor. I raced straight over to the pile, straddled them and lifted up your Grandma's dress to try and cover her butt when Betty comes trotting down the way.

So here I am holding up Grandma's dress looking like I am showing Betty her bum, while she is screaming at Bill, while Susie is flapping like a fish rubbing wet socks in George's face, screaming, 'Don't look! Don't look!' while he's a-waving his arms and legs trying to get out from all of it .... and Betty....Betty, she falls to the ground laughing, laughing so hard she started screaming, 'Stop I'm peeing myself, I'm peeing myself.'"

He can't help himself and starts rocking and roaring again. "What a delightful mess that night was."

A quiet smile replaces the raucous laughter as he wipes his eyes. His gaze shifts beyond the lake as he starts mumbling to himself. "We had such fun together; we sure did, for years we told each other that story."

The boy slowly got up to make coffee, leaving Granddad smiling and nodding to his long passed friends as if they had gathered one last time for the recounting and retelling of their adventures.

As they both settled back into the comfortable silence the old man picked up the story again, but this time it was different, there was a purpose to it.

"The river was high and cold, I think I told you that, and running fast, but we were never worried. We knew that between the six of us we could handle anything thrown at us. You see son, we had

the right people on the boat, we had packed light, and we had each other. We all had our strengths, and we covered for each other's weakness."

"How long did it take you?" the boy asked.

"Two weeks," the old man replied.

"That doesn't seem right; it's only 300 miles by road. I would think it would have been more like a lazy four days by boat."

"We never took the boat, son, we took the raft," he said, waiting for that revelation to sink in.

"You're kidding, that old thing?"

With false dignity, he replied, "Well lad, that old thing is a little bit like the rest of us, she wasn't all that old back then."

"That's not what I mean, Granddad. Why didn't you just take the boat and head down to the coast?"

"Between here and Lewisville are two sets of rapids, and between there and Clarkstown on the coast is another four. At that time of year, the only way to get a raft down the rapids with that many people and supplies is to go around them. If the rapids were too rough or difficult, we would paddle to shore, unpack the raft, carry everything up the riverbank and through the bush and back down to below the rapids. We would then have to repack it all before heading off again. All that takes time and some doing, and we weren't in a hurry."

"That sounds like a lot of effort," the young man said.

"Life takes a lot of effort, son. Getting to where you are supposed to get takes some doing."

The boy smelled the memories of his childhood deeply as his granddad lit his pipe. He said, "There are two types of people in this world - there are raft people, and there are speedboat people - and one day you are going to have to choose which one of those you are going to be."

Without hesitation, the young man said, "I'll take that speed boat any day."

Knowingly the old man smiled, "We all would have at 20, son, we all would have. I know I certainly did. Right up to that trip to Clarkstown."

The boy got concerned and asked, "What happened?"

"Nothing happened, it wasn't like the Deliverance movie or anything."

"What movie?"

"The old Deliverance movie? With the banjos? You've never seen that?"

"No."

"Good, you shouldn't have, it's got some weird stuff in it. Anyways that's not my point; my point is nothing tragic happened. I just

realized something on that trip, and it changed the way I loved your Grandma, and the way I did life from that time on.

I'll be honest, before then, I was a speedboat guy just like you and just like your dad. Always running hard, always charging full steam ahead. Every weekend I would get out on the lake and tear it up, racing from one end to the other as fast as I could. Every summer we would pack the kids up and trailer it down to the coast. We would race around down there for a couple of weeks. It felt great being the 'Captain' of the speedboat. I never thought about the current or the direction of the water. I had all the power; I was in charge, I loved it."

He stood to his feet. "Come walk with me."

As they meandered back down to the dock, he continued to muse.

"You see son, as long as the lake was clear, and I had enough fuel, and there were no obstacles in my way, and the weather was perfect, I could go as fast as I wanted to from here to over there by old Ray's place and back again.

And you see, that was the problem. That was as far as I could go. I was limited by my surroundings. I was limited by fuel. And I was limiting everybody else as well. There was only one person giving input into the direction, me; everyone else just sat there disengaged from the journey, sitting there sightseeing. We might have been in the boat together, but we weren't in the adventure together."

He climbed down the ladder and motioned the young man into the old raft, they cast off and rowed towards the middle of the lake.

They sat there side by side, enveloped by the comfortable silence that comes with a shared life.

"After we got back to the campsite, Susie went off to get changed. We were all sitting there embarrassed and not sure if we should laugh or cry. Susie walked up to us real awkward-like and softly said, 'I'd appreciate it if we never talked about this again.'

Bill got up, put his arms around her, and said very lovingly, 'I understand what Susie is trying to communicate. But just between us 6, I have to say that they are the greatest set of—'

Susie looked at him, horrified, and said in her best Sunday-school-teacher-voice, 'William Thomas!'

'—uh, EYES that I have ever seen and I plan to be looking at them and talking about them for the rest of my life.' It was about 20 minutes before we stopped laughing.

I decided then and there that I wanted to have people around me that I could share the future with. Not just any people, these people. At that moment, I realized how lonely I was and how hard I worked trying to make life happen on my own. I kept everyone at arm's length, even your Grandma, just in case they would try and slow me down.

With a speedboat, we could never have gotten to the coast. We would have probably cracked the hull on the first rapid. People might have gotten hurt, maybe even thrown overboard or even drowned. If we had made it over the first rapid without smashing the hull, at some point we would have run out of fuel. I might have

been the sole captain of the boat, but what is the use of being the captain of a sinking ship or a ship that's going nowhere?"

As they rowed back towards shore he continued:

"The raft was different; we were all in this together. As a group, we decided what gear we needed for the trip. We all rowed together, pulling towards a common goal, yet we were going with the flow of the river, following the current. It's not like we didn't have control, we just trusted that the river knew where it was going, and we weren't trying to fight it by rowing in the opposite direction. If we hit a difficulty, a challenge, like the rapids or debris, we all had input as to whether or not we thought we could make it. If we didn't think we could, we all got involved carrying our gear and the raft up and over as I told you. We did the hard work together, and we enjoyed the reward of the drifting and coasting with the current together as well."

The warm glow of the afternoon sun washed over them reassuringly as they pottered around on the dock putting everything back, ready for the next time they would need it. As they stood there admiring their work, Granddad stopped and in an uncustomary act of intimacy, pulled the young man to himself. He kissed him on the cheek, and held him long enough for the awkwardness of rare affection to fade and be replaced by the precious unspoken bond of love that grown men share but rarely talk of.

"Jack, your Daddy was a special man, one of those rare combinations of both big dreamer and passionate doer. My one regret concerning him was that I never got to tell him about my trip and my thoughts on the raft and the speedboat. He never had enough time to stop to hear me, and I never made a point of sharing it. Then one day

it was too late. I sometimes wonder if I had, then maybe he would have slowed down long enough to take a holiday, and maybe he would never have died that day."

"Don't be like that Granddad, that's not fair to you."

"This isn't a pity party son, not at all. I stopped throwing those years ago. Besides, there is no room on the raft for extra baggage. No, this isn't extra baggage, this is my one bag. This is the one thing I have chosen to carry all these years, and today I give it to you.

I'm not giving you the pain of burying a child. Grandma and I dealt with that one together, and I put it to rest with her. What I want to give you is this story of the raft and the speedboat. It is the thing I have held in my heart for 40 years, the gift I wanted to give to your Dad is now yours.

Son, every man, at some point in his life, will be faced with the same choice I was. Will you limit yourself to being the captain of a speedboat, or will you take a chance on your friends and family, and go with the flow of life and stop fighting it? With everything that's in me, I pray that you will be the sort of man who trusts that God Himself knows where the river of your life is destined to flow, and you will row with Him not against Him."

## FINAL REMARKS

I don't know what is next, but I trust in the One who through it all has loved me. The One who knew me at my worst, but chose only to see me as if I were at my best. I've got my best friend at my side, my life partner, someone more than capable of pulling an oar and sharing the load. And I trust that this river that is our life adventure will take us to where we are supposed to go.

This is not the life I would have planned for or wanted for myself, but it is the life I have been given, and I am grateful for it. Instead of being ashamed of it or scared by it, I have come to accept my life and love it as my own.

Mel and I only hope and sincerely pray that those of you who have been through the worst of it will allow it to bring out the best in you.

We wish you Peace and Much Grace for your journey ahead. Relax, you're going to make it.

John and Melissa

# APPLIED PSYCHOLOGICAL METHODOLOGIES/PATHWAYS

# (JOHN'S TOOLBOX)

For those of you who want to go deeper into recovery from trauma, our great friend and editor, Kathysue Dorey has managed to outline the tools/competencies used by John throughout the book. She was amazed at how many methodologies he taught himself intuitively through independent study and problem-solving. We've included those in a table on the following pages.

For more information and resources for using #dealwithit in your small group, therapy or training setting, or to have John speak or train at your organization, please email me: **dealwithit@ nextfoundation.org.**

—Melissa

| | CHRONOLOGICAL CONTEXT | TOOLBOX APPLICATION |
|---|---|---|
| Dedication | 2017 | The attribute of Gratitude |
| Introduction | | |
| A Beginning of Sorts | 2017 | The attributes of Humor and Perspective |
| | | The power of Storytelling |
| | | The competency of Optimism |
| Tuck Your Chin and Throw Punches | 2010 | The attribute of Courage |
| | | The leadership trait of Resilience |
| | | The affective skill of Sensing Gaps |
| | | The affective skill of Tolerance for Risks |
| Chapter 1: The Story So Far | | |
| Oh Crap What Have I Done?! | May 2017 | The creativity skill of Look At It Another Way |
| | Flashback to 1967 | The attribute of Bravery |
| | | The competency of Stress Tolerance |
| When the Walls Came Tumbling Down | 2008 | The competency of Reality Testing |
| | The 'Sausage Debacle' in 2014 | The affective skill of Mindfulness |
| | | The competency of Emotional Self Awareness |
| Re-defining Normal | Began in 2009 | The power of Storytelling |
| | Contemplation of suicide in 2009 and 2010 | The Affirmative Environment |
| | Began in 2010 | The beginning practice of Challenge the Process |

| METHODOLOGY/PATHWAY | CITATION |
| --- | --- |
| Positive Psychology | Peterson and Seligman (2004) |
| | page 19 |
| Positive Psychology | Peterson and Seligman (2004) |
| The Disney Creative Strategy | Dilts (1994) |
| EQi 2.0 | MHS, Inc. (2011) |
| Positive Psychology | Peterson and Seligman (2004) |
| The Truth About Leadership | Kouzes & Posner (2010) |
| Thinking Skills Model | Puccio, Mance & Murdock (2011) |
| Thinking Skills Model | Puccio, Mance & Murdock (2011) |
| | page 27 |
| Making the Leap Beyond | Torrance and Safter (1998) |
| Positive Psychology | Peterson and Seligman (2004) |
| EQi 2.0 | MHS, Inc. (2011) |
| EQi 2.0 | MHS, Inc. (2011) |
| Thinking Skills Model | Puccio, Mance & Murdock (2011) |
| EQi 2.0 | MHS, Inc. (2011) |
| The Disney Creative Strategy | Dilts (1994) |
| Creative Problem-Solving | Miller, Firestien, Vehar (2007) |
| The Leadership Challenge | Kouzes & Posner (2007) |

343

| | CHRONOLOGICAL CONTEXT | TOOLBOX APPLICATION |
|---|---|---|
| | | The creativity skill of Breakthrough-Expand the Boundaries |
| | | The thinking skills of Ideational and Visionary Thinking |
| | | The affective skill of Sensitivity to Environment |
| | Filmed Stopping Traffic documentary in 2015 | The competency of Social Responsibility |
| Now What? | Year span 2012-2015 | The practice of Challenge the Process |
| | | The thinking skills of Tactical, Contextual and Evaluative Thinking |
| | | The stages of Formulating a Plan and Formulating Solutions |
| | | The creativity skills of Be Flexible and Put Your Ideas In Context |
| Mel's Turn | The acceptance of risk taking | The affective skill of Avoiding Premature Closure |
| | | The Affirmative Environment |
| Chapter 2: Never a Victim | | |
| Never a Victim | 'Never a Victim' poem was written in 2012 | The leadership trait of Accountability |
| | Therapy with Mona was in 2013 | The competency of Interpersonal Relationships |
| | | The attributes of Humor and Love of Learning |
| | | The creativity skill of Keep Open |

| METHODOLOGY/PATHWAY | CITATION |
| --- | --- |
| Making the Leap Beyond | Torrance and Safter (1998) |
| Thinking Skills Model | Puccio, Mance & Murdock (2011) |
| Thinking Skills Model | Puccio, Mance & Murdock (2011) |
| EQi 2.0 | MHS, Inc. (2011) |
| The Leadership Challenge | Kouzes & Posner (2007) |
| Thinking Skills Model | Puccio, Mance & Murdock (2011) |
| Thinking Skills Model | Puccio, Mance & Murdock (2011) |
| Making the Leap Beyond | Torrance and Safter (1998) |
| Thinking Skills Model | Puccio, Mance & Murdock (2011) |
| Creative Problem-Solving | Miller, Firestien, Vehar (2007) |
| The Leadership Challenge | Kouzes & Posner (2007) |
| EQi 2.0 | MHS, Inc. (2011) |
| Positive Psychology | Peterson and Seligman (2004) |
| Making the Leap Beyond | Torrance and Safter (1998) |

page 59

| | CHRONOLOGICAL CONTEXT | TOOLBOX APPLICATION |
|---|---|---|
| | | The SAVI Approach |
| | | The competency of Self Regard |
| You Might be Right, I Might be Crazy | Study and research was in 2016 and 2017 regarding the stigma, shame and lies surrounding boys, men and sexual abuse; along with understanding the nature of mental illness. | The thinking skill of Strategic Thinking |
| | | The practice of Encourage the Heart |
| | | The value of Kindness |
| The Victim Narrative | Ongoing since the late 1990's | The practice of Model the Way |
| | | The value of Self Regulation |
| | | The competency of Self Actualization |
| | | The power of Positivity |
| Mel's Turn | The power of commitment | The Affirmative Environment |
| Chapter 3: Kangaroos in the Top Paddock | | |
| Kangaroos in the Top Paddock | 2016, Atlanta business meeting | The affective skill of Playfulness |
| | An understanding of the nature of PTSD | The thinking skill of Diagnostic Thinking |
| Frontal Lobe, Frontal Lobe Wherefore Art Thou | How the brain rewires itself for function after trauma and the nature of suicide | The step of Assessing the Situation |
| | | The innate ability to be creative |
| | 2016 - The Sailing Incident and impact of my personal high-risk behavior on others | The practice of Metacognition |
| Mel's Turn | The value of love and a smile | The Affirmative Environment |

| METHODOLOGY/PATHWAY | CITATION |
| --- | --- |
| Accelerated Learning | David Meier (2000) |
| EQi 2.0 | MHS, Inc. (2011) |
| Thinking Skills Model | Puccio, Mance & Murdock (2011) |
| The Leadership Challenge | Kouzes & Posner (2007) |
| Positive Psychology | Peterson and Seligman (2004) |
| The Leadership Challenge | Kouzes & Posner (2007) |
| Positive Psychology | Peterson and Seligman (2004) |
| EQi 2.0 | MHS, Inc. (2011) |
| The Truth About Leadership | Kouzes & Posner (2010) |
| The Truth About Leadership | Kouzes & Posner (2010) |
| | page 95 |
| Thinking Skills Model | Puccio, Mance & Murdock (2011) |
| Thinking Skills Model | Puccio, Mance & Murdock (2011) |
| Thinking Skills Model | Puccio, Mance & Murdock (2011) |
| Creativity in Genius | Stein (1983) |
| Metaphysics | Aristotle (350 BCE) |
| Positive Psychology | Peterson and Seligman (2004) |

| | CHRONOLOGICAL CONTEXT | TOOLBOX APPLICATION |
|---|---|---|
| **Chapter 4: Living from the Inside-Out** | | |
| Living from the Inside-Out | Began in 2009-2010 | The affective skill of Dreaming |
| | Re-evaluated and re-applied in 2016 | The construct of Authenticity |
| | How to change the way I think | The stage of Explore the Challenge |
| | | The Growth Mindset |
| The Magical Number Seven Plus or Minus Two | 2009-2010 | The power of Positivity |
| | Utilizing the unconscious for gains in the conscious world | The effectiveness of Positive Affirmations |
| Rebooting My System | Bodybuilding, 2015-2016 | The competency of Independence |
| | The nature of self-sabotage | The practice of Failing Forward and Miss-takes |
| | Head and heart in the game, 2015 to present | The value of Persistence |
| | The research on heart memory, 2010 | The power of the Human Heart |
| Me and My Superpower | Understanding the nature of the brain, 2013 | The creativity skill of Be Aware of Emotions |
| Stress to Strength | Return to Australia in 2012 | The competency of Emotional Expression |
| | | The creativity skill of Combine and Synthesize |
| Mel's Turn | The value of unconditional support | The Affirmative Environment |
| **Chapter 5: The Tale of Two Men** | | |
| The Tale of Two Men | Shadow of a Man poem was written in 2011 | The creativity skill of Be Original |

| METHODOLOGY/PATHWAY | CITATION |
|---|---|
| | page 119 |
| Thinking Skills Model | Puccio, Mance & Murdock (2011) |
| Let Your Life Speak | Palmer (2000) |
| Creative Problem-Solving | Miller, Firestien, Vehar (2007) |
| Mindset: The New Psychology of Success | Dweck (2006) |
| The Truth About Leadership | Kouzes & Posner (2010) |
| Positive Affirmations | Mitchell (2014) |
| EQi 2.0 | MHS, Inc. (2011) |
| The 21 Irrefutable Laws of Leadership | Maxwell ( 2007 ) |
| Positive Psychology | Peterson and Seligman (2004) |
| The Truth About Leadership | Kouzes & Posner (2010) |
| Making the Leap Beyond | Torrance and Safter (1998) |
| EQi 2.0 | MHS, Inc. (2011) |
| Making the Leap Beyond | Torrance and Safter (1998) |
| Creative Problem-Solving | Miller, Firestien, Vehar (2007) |
| | page 155 |
| Making the Leap Beyond | Torrance and Safter (1998) |

| | CHRONOLOGICAL CONTEXT | TOOLBOX APPLICATION |
|---|---|---|
| | Concept and acceptance of John 2.0, 2011 | The value of Acceptance |
| | The home show was 2017. The concept of Change-ability as opposed to Dis-ability occurred to me in 2017. | The importance of Embracing Change |
| You Are Not a Beautiful or Unique Snowflake | Re-read biographies in 2008 and looking at old knowledge with fresh eyes to see new things. | The creativity skill of Look At It Another Way |
| | | The thinking skill of Diagnostic Thinking |
| | There is no secret to success | The practice of Thinking Outside of the Box |
| Thoughts are Things | 2010-2011 - The power of my thoughts to create my future. | The step of Exploring the Vision |
| | The power of personal history | The commitment to Experiment and Take Risks |
| Three Things I Needed to Deal With | #1 Honor your Mother and Father, 2010 | The creativity skill of The Problem |
| | Australia 2012. First discussion with my sister and the attempted grooming of my son by my parents for abuse happened during this trip. | The power of Letting Go |
| | #2 Guilt vs Conscience, 2016-2017 | |
| | #3 All women are lying... | The attribute of Appreciation of Beauty and Excellence |
| | Flashback to first occasion of oral sex, 1967 | The competencies of Reality Testing, Impulse Control and Stress Tolerance |

| METHODOLOGY/PATHWAY | CITATION |
|---|---|
| The Last Lecture | Pausch (2008) |
| Transformational Leadership | Burns (2003) |
| Making the Leap Beyond | Torrance and Safter (1998) |
| Thinking Skills Model | Puccio, Mance & Murdock (2011) |
| Creative Problem-Solving | Miller, Firestien, Vehar (2007) |
| Thinking Skills Model | Puccio, Mance & Murdock (2011) |
| The Leadership Challenge | Kouzes & Posner (2007) |
| Making the Leap Beyond | Torrance and Safter (1998) |
| The Last Lecture | Pausch (2008) |
| Positive Psychology | Peterson and Seligman (2004) |
| EQi 2.0 | MHS, Inc. (2011) |

| | CHRONOLOGICAL CONTEXT | TOOLBOX APPLICATION |
|---|---|---|
| | Parties and filming, early 1970's | |
| | Interrogation by feminist academia, 1974 | |
| | I wrote 'Do You See Him Now' in 2017 | |
| Mel's Turn | The value of Strength of Character | The Affirmative Environment |
| **Chapter 6: From Knowing Someone to Being Someone** | | |
| From Knowing Someone to Being Someone | Began in 2009 the development of Information, Revelation, Application, Transformation | The four creative preference styles: Clarifier, Ideator, Developer, Implementor |
| How to Reprogram Your Mind | The development programs were in 2009-2012 and I revisited them in 2015 | Embracing Failure and Mistakes |
| | The first 7 Actionable Steps (part 1) -- The Brains Trust and Relational Asset Inventory | The self enforced Role Play |
| | | The practice of Enable Others to Act: Foster Collaboration |
| | | The continued affective skills of Dreaming and Mindfulness |
| | | The attribute of Trust |
| | The Mental Detox Program with 10 more Actionable Steps (part 2) | The competencies of Interpersonal Relationships and Assertiveness |
| | | The application of Metacognition |
| | | The value of Self Motivation |
| | | Set yourself up for success |

| METHODOLOGY/PATHWAY | CITATION |
|---|---|
| | |
| Creative Problem-Solving | Miller, Firestien, Vehar (2007) |
| | page 199 |
| Foursight Thinking Profile® | Puccio (2014) |
| Learning to Lead | Bennis and Goldsmith (1997) |
| Sociodrama | Moreno (1943) |
| The Leadership Challenge | Kouzes & Posner (2007) |
| Thinking Skills Model | Puccio, Mance & Murdock (2011) |
| The Truth About Leadership | Kouzes & Posner (2010) |
| EQi 2.0 | MHS, Inc. (2011) |
| Metacognition | Dunlosky and Metcalfe (2008) |
| Life's Greatest Lessons | Urban (2003) |
| Coach Wooden's Leadership Game | Wooden and Jamison (2009) |

| | CHRONOLOGICAL CONTEXT | TOOLBOX APPLICATION |
|---|---|---|
| Mel's Turn | Positive follows positive | The Affirmative Environment |
| **Chapter 7: Happiness, Unicorns and Other Myths** | | |
| What is Happiness? Defining and Rating Happiness | Research on happiness began in 2013 | Putting it all together into the Well-being Indicator: |
| | The 5 Principles of Unhappiness | Self Regard, Optimism, Self Actualization, Interpersonal Relationships |
| Getting to Happy | 5 Critical Thoughts of Happiness | Putting it all together into the Well-being Indicator: |
| | My Conclusions: The Happiness Model | Self Regard, Optimism, Self Actualization, Interpersonal Relationships |
| Mel's Turn | Little Miss Sunshine | The Affirmative Environment |
| **Chapter 8: This is Going to Hurt** | | |
| This is Going to Hurt | 2010, dealing with bitterness, forgiveness and lack of trust | The attributes of Forgiveness and Mercy |
| | | The benefit of Positive Affirmations |
| | The Spreadsheet of love | The affective skill of Playfulness |
| Afflicted or Infected | 2015, confronting the myths about forgiveness and learning to walk in forgiveness not bitterness; practicing for confrontation and discussion | The practice of Encourage the Heart: Celebrate the values and victories; create a spirit of Community, be personally involved |
| | | The practice of Inspire a Shared Vision |
| | | The importance of Role Playing |
| Uncluttering My Soul | 2015, I am not my past, I am my future | The benefit of Resilience |

| METHODOLOGY/PATHWAY | CITATION |
|---|---|
| Creative Problem-Solving | Miller, Firestien, Vehar (2007) |
| | page 225 |
| EQi 2.0 | MHS, Inc. (2011) |
| EQi 2.0 | MHS, Inc. (2011) |
| The Happiness Model | adapted from Etcoff and King (2017) |
| Creative Problem-Solving | Miller, Firestien, Vehar (2007) |
| | page 255 |
| Positive Psychology | Peterson and Seligman (2004) |
| The Truth About Leadership | Kouzes & Posner (2010) |
| Thinking Skills Model | Puccio, Mance & Murdock (2011) |
| The Leadership Challenge | Kouzes & Posner (2007) |
| The Leadership Challenge | Kouzes & Posner (2007) |
| Sociodrama | Moreno (1943) |
| The Truth About Leadership | Kouzes & Posner (2010) |

| | CHRONOLOGICAL CONTEXT | TOOLBOX APPLICATION |
|---|---|---|
| | The 6 Myths of Forgiveness | The step of Formulating Challenges |
| | The 4 Truths of Forgiveness | The thinking skill of Tactical Thinking |
| Mel's Turn | The importance of reflection | The Affirmative Environment |
| **Chapter 9: Love and Other Bruises** | | |
| Let's Talk About Sex | 2017, The Sex Survey | The practice of Encourage the Heart: recognize contributions by showing appreciation for individual excellence |
| | | The attributes of Hope and Fairness |
| The Power of a Partner | 2015 until forever | |
| | The "I see you" principal | The creativity skill of Highlight the Essence |
| | My wife is not my caregiver | The attribute of Personal Responsibility |
| | 3 issues in all marriages: Communication, Sex and Money | The importance of shared values that drive commitment |
| | | The creativity skill of Let Humor Flow and Use It |
| | The difference between a PTSD incident and an episode | The practice of Situational Awareness |
| Random Questions from Randomer Friends | | The power of Vulnerability |
| Mel's Turn | The gift of our marriage | The Affirmative Environment |

| METHODOLOGY/PATHWAY | CITATION |
|---|---|
| Thinking Skills Model | Puccio, Mance & Murdock (2011) |
| Thinking Skills Model | Puccio, Mance & Murdock (2011) |
| Creative Problem-Solving | Miller, Firestien, Vehar (2007) |
| The Leadership Challenge | Kouzes & Posner (2007) |
| Positive Psychology | Peterson and Seligman (2004) |
| Making the Leap Beyond | Torrance and Safter (1998) |
| The Truth About Leadership | Kouzes & Posner (2010) |
| The Truth About Leadership | Kouzes & Posner (2010) |
| Making the Leap Beyond | Torrance and Safter (1998) |
| Pure Krav Maga: Self Defense Mastery (™) | Boaz Aviram (2014) |
| The Power of Vulnerability | Brown (2013) |
| Creative Problem-Solving | Miller, Firestien, Vehar (2007) |

page 289

| | CHRONOLOGICAL CONTEXT | TOOLBOX APPLICATION |
|---|---|---|
| **Epilogue** | | |
| What's Next | 2017 | The affective skill of Tolerance for Risks |
| The Raft and the Speedboat | 2016 | The gift of Spirituality |
| Last Remarks | 2017 | The attribute of Humility |

| METHODOLOGY/PATHWAY | CITATION |
|---|---|
| | page 321 |
| Thinking Skills Model | Puccio, Mance & Murdock (2011) |
| Mother Teresa | Chawla (1997) |
| Positive Psychology | Peterson and Seligman (2004) |

## MORE FROM DR. JOHN A. KING

Read more from Dr. King in his selection of raw, unflinching poetry published during the beginning stages of his recovery. *No Working Title: a Life in Progress* explores the effects of sexual abuse and pornography on boys as they grow into manhood. All proceeds benefit those who are sexually abused or trafficked.

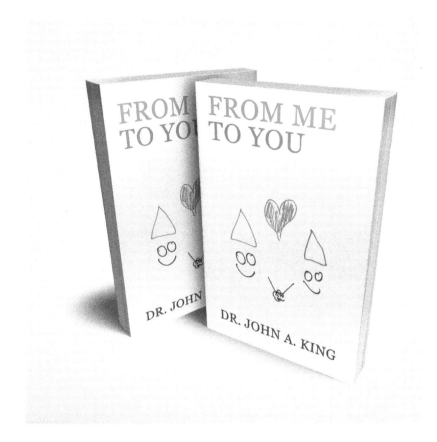

**COMING SOON!!**

Poems about love...

AVAILABLE FALL 2018 ON
WWW.DRJOHNAKING.COM